The Essential Guide for The Married Man

The Essential Guide for The Married Man

Principles and Lessons for Navigating a Successful Marriage and a Meaningful Life

E. Paul Allerton

Waterside Productions

Waterside Productions
2055 Oxford Ave.
Cardiff, CA 92007

ISBN-13: 978-1-951805-26-5

Visit themarriedman.net

Table of Contents

Chapter Two – Getting Ready

Chapter Three – Just Married!

Chapter Six – The Golden Years

Chapter Seven – What Men Should Know About Women

Acknowledgements

More than anyone, I wish to thank my wife Nancy for tolerating and loving me for more than 35 years now. It wasn't easy for her, particularly in the beginning, when I really didn't know what I was doing. She was, is, and continues to be the co-pilot in my development and she has suffered through the many mishaps of my learning.

I also wish to acknowledge John Testaverde, a good friend without whom this book would still be just a figment of my imagination. I also thank the following men: Roger Poor, Scott Humbert, Don Todrin, David Macey, among many, who contributed time and energy to research, edit, correct, and counsel me in my efforts.

I acknowledge the giants of this field: Dr. James Dobson, Mark Gruber, Chuck Swindoll, Dr. Larry Crabb, Gary Smalley, John Trent and countless others who blazed the trail and provided me with much of the insights, perspectives, and lessons embodied within this text. Without these, I would have crashed my ship among the treacherous rocks of selfishness, doubt, and resignation. Instead I have enjoyed some of the very best fruits of being married for more than three decades.

Lastly, I wish to thank Alex, a young man who rediscovered hope for himself from reading an early, unpublished edition of this text, which compelled me to finish what I had started. This is my hope for you: that you embrace, learn, and master the mindset and mission to be a great husband, and that in doing so you will discover more than you can imagine.

Introduction

"We make a living by what we get,
but we make a life by what we give."
unknown

Marriage and becoming a father are two of the most important *Rites of Passage* in a man's life. Unfortunately, our society no longer recognizes them as such, nor do the elder men prepare, counsel, and train the younger men to succeed in these endeavors. Furthermore, there are desperately few elder men who are adequately equipped and possess the conviction to do so. As a result, good men and women enter marriage with false expectations and misconceptions about how to create a successful marriage. Flawed from the start, their marriage can gradually drift off course and all too often fails despite the best efforts and good intentions of both parties. Worse, hiding behind the veil of 'no-fault divorce', neither party has the courage to take responsibility for their part in the failure; no one is accountable for their actions.

Consequently, a growing number of men today, paralyzed by their insecurity and afraid that they might fail, avoid the risk, opting to forgo marriage altogether. Regrettably, these men wind up either alone, dating multiple women, or loitering in prolonged relationships void of any serious commitment, direction, or future. It is increasingly common for a man simply to live with a woman for a decade without providing any real sense of direction, only to wake up years later empty, unfulfilled, and less than the man he knows he could have been. For their part, all too many women opt to live with a man before marriage hoping that he will someday commit, but they've removed all incentives to do so. When their relationship ends, these women have wasted their most valuable years and sabotaged their ability to get married and have a family. Giving in to the hurt of this experience, they can become bitter, untrusting, and leery of the men in their future relationships.

Statistics on marriage and divorce rates are surprisingly stale and incomplete. The US Center for Disease Control (CDC), which tracks various U.S. health statistics in the National Vital Statistics System, is three years delayed. The CDC's data show that U.S. marriage rates have declined slightly more than 20% from 8.2 per thousand in 2000 to 6.5 per thousand in 2018. For the same period, the divorce rate has also dropped marginally in line with fewer marriages, but continues to negatively affect more than 32% of all US marriages. This is likely understated because data from California, Georgia, Hawaii, Indiana, Louisiana, and Minnesota are not included.[1]

The financial cost of divorce is also staggering. Fees paid to divorce attorneys' range between $15,000 to $30,000, representing a $28 billion dollar industry. And that's just the beginning. The cost to maintain two households, instead of one, cheats the average divorced family of another $20,000 or more annually. The financial costs, while significant, pale compared to the long-term emotional and psychological costs to the divorced couple and worse, to the innocent victims, their children. Contrary to what divorcees would like to believe, extensive research over the past thirty years continues to confirm that children are emotionally worse off five years after the divorce than on the day of the divorce. Studies report: Children from divorced homes suffer academically, are substantially more likely to be incarcerated for committing a crime as a juvenile, are almost five times more likely to live in poverty, are much more likely to engage in drug and alcohol use as well as sexual intercourse, experience illness more frequently and recover from sickness more slowly, and suffer more frequently from symptoms of psychological distress.[2]

---

[1] https://www.cdc.gov/nchs/nvss/marriage-divorce.htm?CDC_AA_refVal=https%3A%2F%2Fwww.cdc.gov%2Fnchs%2Fmardiv.htm

[2] http://www.focusonthefamily.com/marriage/divorce-and-infidelity/should-i-get-a-divorce/how-could-divorce-affect-my-kids#fn5

One participant in the late psychologist Judith Wallerstein's 25-year study of the consequences of divorce on children, sums it up:

"Children never get over divorce.
It is a great loss that is in their lives forever. It is like a grief that is never over. All special events, such as holidays, plays, sports, graduations, marriages, births of children, etc., bring up the loss created by divorce as well as the family relationship conflicts that result from the 'extended family' celebrating any event."

Whether you are decidedly single, contemplating marriage, married, or divorced, this book provides you with powerful insights and perspectives necessary for you to not just survive in your marriage, but to THRIVE in it. I seek to help you experience the very best that can come from a man and a woman taking that important journey into marriage and allowing that commitment to shape and mold you into the best man you can be: for yourself, for your wife, for your children, and for your community.

The book is organized as a reference guide. There are chapters for the major stages of life, and found within each chapter is a set of key principles that are important to that stage. For each one, I provide short paragraphs with key insights on that topic, enough to move you in the right direction. There are whole books on many of these topics, deservedly so, and I have provided pointers to those I have found useful. This format is easy to digest and allows you to quickly find the information that you seek. You don't have to invest a great deal of time and effort to extract great value from it as a reference guide. However, I challenge you to seek to understand and make the necessary connections between the concepts to uncover the powerful synergies available from these principles. Commit yourself to embrace and master each of the many lessons within. Each principle has the power to transform your perspective and as a result change the quality of your life and the lives of those you care for. Just like a great temple, the more pillars you master, the stronger and more blessed your marriage will be.

This book covers a lot of ground. It begins with important perspectives to embrace before you even begin, and then navigates through some of the common stages and struggles of marriage. In this way, you can view this book as a map to help you navigate the hills and valleys, majestic peaks and treacherous caverns of marriage. While you may be drawn to the chapter that addresses your current situation, read the chapters in succession to take advantage of the organized building blocks that will properly prepare you for the road ahead.

In the text that follows, I draw from and reference the excellent efforts of many men who have come before me. It is my hope that this book guides you to other texts and resources to further your understanding. If you are facing a specific challenge or find a particular concept insightful, I encourage you, ***no, I exhort you***, to follow the references or use the resource guide in the appendix to further aid your quest to understand, apply, and master these concepts.

If you are a man who readily accepts the counsel of the successful men who have come before you, then you will get immediate value from this one book alone. However, if you are a "Doubting Thomas", a man who needs undeniable evidence and proof before you are willing to accept a new principle or perspective, then I dare you to follow the references to other texts where much of the research and supporting evidence can be found.

All the topics are important. I ask my children, "What is the easiest mess to clean up?" to which they have been trained to reply, "The one that I don't make!" One of the best ways to minimize the future risk of conflict in your marriage is to:

Understand what causes conflicts and the best ways to respond.

Ideally, you will learn how to avoid conflict altogether. Hint: Don't wait until you are in a major crisis before you start developing the skills, insights, and experiences necessary to navigate, resolve, and eliminate such conflicts. My goal is not that you struggle through your marriage, but that you are transformed by it, so that you, your wife, and most importantly your children, experience the joy of being in an emotionally strong, loving, and nurturing family. So, read the whole book in any order you like, but read the whole book, and then read it again!

In the beginning, you may have an intellectual or perhaps social objection to the key messages presented in this book. Until you implement a principle, your objections would be based only on your opinion and most likely not on your experience. You can dismiss this text as generalizations or you may foolishly think your situation is unique or special. It isn't. You must be willing to suspend your opinion of what you read until you have applied the principles and lessons for 90 days diligently. After 90 days you will begin to have experiences that you won't be able to dismiss or deny. It takes a minimum of 90 days to develop a new habit and to change your behavior. Commit yourself to applying any new concepts or principles for 90 days before you allow yourself to have an opinion on it. Otherwise you may look for evidence that it is not true and then use that as an excuse to ignore its benefit to you. Dare to seek evidence that it is true!

Be forewarned, I present a masculine, intentionally hard hitting, and deliberately unapologetic view. I assure you, there will be topics and perspectives contained herein that you will resist and perhaps vehemently fight against. Notice that your reaction is largely a defensive mechanism against accepting responsibility for the pain and anguish you may have caused the ones you love. For your sake and for those you care the most about, I challenge you to push forward and read the entire text. My intent is not to cause you harm, but if needed, this book may open old wounds that have festered for decades and never healed. Have the courage to accept that this view may be closer to the truth than your own 'story' and rip open the wound, extract the pus, and let yourself be transformed, healed, and strengthened.

In the pages ahead I will make bold and challenging statements. Depending on your personal situation, you may find some quite difficult. Don't take these personally or use them as an excuse to reject the lessons. Challenge yourself to make it personal by reflecting on what can or will be different if you accept them as true. Have the courage to objectively find the evidence that the traces of truth exist. The trap that you may fall into is that when another man challenges your behavior or character, you think he is doing something TO you. A secure man welcomes and understands that the man is doing something FOR you. The Book of Proverbs is full of powerful insights and counsel for men. Proverbs 27:17 states, "As iron sharpens iron, So a man sharpens the countenance of his friend." And Proverbs 12:1, "Whoever loves instruction loves knowledge, but he who hates correction is stupid." And finally, Proverbs 19:25 offers, "Strike a scoffer, and the simple will become wary; Rebuke one who has understanding, and he will discern knowledge."

Warning! If you have been off track or operating with false assumptions for some time, it may take your marriage some time to turn things around and a little bit longer to be healthy and vibrant. Be patient, the fruits are worth waiting for and I promise you they will be ever so sweet.

The measure of a man is his willingness to be responsible for that which he is not responsible for!

To get maximum value from this book, you must have the courage to take full personal responsibility for the state of your marriage and your life. No blame, no excuses, no justifications, no rationalizations, just *100% responsibility* for where you are and where you are going as you put these principles to work in your life.

Finally, I confess, the text that follows contains very few original thoughts. Most of the principles have been around a long time. But I present the concepts with fresh vision so you can readily apply them. They are packaged in a fashion that tie the pieces together for greater understanding. The goal is that you develop confidence as you navigate your way forward.

You may not have grown up with the leadership of a strong father who taught you how to care for a woman. If you didn't, this book will be particularly helpful. Many who have had good examples have dismissed them as being old-fashioned and no longer relevant in today's culture. Still others lack the confidence that they can live up to that example. If you commit to mastering the attitude and skills of a married man and to honorably serving your family, you will profoundly enhance the quality of your life, your family, and the community as a whole. Let the journey begin!

Remember, when navigating the turbulent seas of life, you can't adjust the wind, but you can adjust your sails. I hope this prepares you to get the most from your life.

Chapter One - Before You Begin

"If you don't know where you are going
any road will take you there!"
- Lewis Carroll

The Fall of the Masculine Culture

We live in a world where when a man turns 18 or 21 he is thrown into the ocean and on his own he eventually drowns. Contrast that to tribal cultures where when a man became of age he was taken and received by the men of the tribe. This Rite of Passage was profound in many ways. Instead of being abandoned, he was received. With this sense of belonging he earned his place among the men of the tribe. In this environment he developed trust, and the men provided instruction, counsel, and the right amount of challenge to propel him forward. What it meant to be a man and everything that a man needed to know was painstakingly passed down from generation to generation. The older men were invested in -- and had a vested interest in -- the development and survival of the younger men. The tribe survived and thrived because of this interdependence.

This environment was rich in experiences, learning, and development. Men learn in four ways. By the experience of success, the tragic pain of failure, watching other men fail, and trusting the counsel of the respected elder. Trusting the counsel of elder men is essential to a man's development. Contrast that to today where men are left to fend for themselves. Without a proper foundation, they can be paralyzed with doubt and insecurity. Worse yet, instead of being respected, what it means to be a man is being marginalized and labeled as "toxic masculinity." Far too few men have any older men as role models to provide them counsel and guidance, and when they do, all too many reject it. Meanwhile young women are being celebrated at every corner. It is very politically correct to hold a "Women in Power" conference, but you'll hear 'men in power' should be abolished. What is a young man to believe?

To what do you belong? Where is your place among men? And who provides you with perspective and counsel? Whom do you trust and whom do you rely on? To whom are you accountable? If you can answer any of these questions with confidence, then you are a lucky man in today's society.

Know Where YOU are Going!

Before a man contemplates inviting a woman, any woman for that matter, into his life to begin a serious relationship and to become his wife for the rest of his life, he ***must*** know where he is going and be on his way to going there! The older he gets, the clearer he should be and the further along his path he should be. Yet all too few stop to ask and answer this question for themselves: *Where am I going and what is my life about?* Have you?

In *Men are from Mars, Women are from Venus*, John Gray (Gray, 1992) refers to men as trains in a train station and each train has its own destination. If the train (man) is clear about where it is going, then the *right* woman will get on the train. However, if the train is ambiguous about where it is going or worse isn't going anywhere at all, then the *wrong* woman may get on, and when the man finally figures out where he really intends to go, he has a serious problem. Worse, if a man projects that he is going one place and then changes his mind and goes somewhere else, he has deceived the woman altogether.

More than what your career is or what your hobbies and interests are, do you know: Who you are? What you value? What you ***stand for***? Have you sorted out what your time on this planet is and will be about? Do you know what is worth living for and what is worth dying for? Really? These are central questions you must answer before you get too tangled up with a woman who may lead you astray or cause you to compromise your mission. Until a man knows what he would die for, he never really understands what he is living for. So, if you've never asked yourself these questions, *it is time to start leading yourself and your life forward*. If you are uncertain of your answers, ***it's time to choose*** and step forward.

I often tease men about the good news about turning forty, because once a man turns forty, he has the physical experience that his life is half over, at least the productive years. So I exhort them to figure out what their life is about so they can *'get on with it'*. Otherwise, they just might get to the end of their life only to realize they have failed in their mission, that their life lacked meaning and purpose. As the Cheshire Cat responds in *Alice in Wonderland*, "***If you don't know where you're going, any road will get you there.***" Wayne Dyer charges people with these words: *"Don't die with your music inside."* Perhaps it is time for you to choose your path!

Purpose

Purpose provides your life direction and it is your way of answering the questions why you are here and what your life is about. Serving your chosen purpose will require you to develop discipline and determination. In Chapter 7 of his book, *The Way of the Superior Man*, David Deida advocates that *"Your purpose must come before your relationship."* All too many men neglect to accept the responsibility to claim and serve a purpose; instead they adopt a laissez-faire attitude and believe that their life is about them and that they should be happy. Let me assure you, nobody really cares if you are happy, except perhaps your mother, if you are lucky.

A man's purpose is not given; it must be *chosen*. When a man claims for himself his purpose, he is making a declaration about what he can be counted on for and who can count on him. And herein lies the magic: once you accept that someone or something is counting on you, it draws you forward. It pulls you past where you would otherwise quit on your own. If a man isn't up to anything, then it doesn't matter if he gives his best! He is irrelevant. However, in order to fulfill your purpose, that requires your best. You must organize your life so that you can be counted on; you must claim your purpose. Then you must develop the character needed to serve your purpose. Deep down all men aspire to be a man that other men respect. More on this later in this chapter.

Purpose brings meaning to your life. In the words of George Washington: "Human happiness and moral duty are inseparably connected." Purpose is the "WHY" in your life, the reason you make sacrifices and keep your agreements. My favorite definition of sacrifice is: forgoing something valued for the sake of something having a more pressing claim. A man must decide what has a more pressing claim on his life and what he is willing to forgo to serve that. Your purpose can serve any cause that will benefit others. When choosing a purpose, don't overcomplicate it with some lofty words which sound good but are difficult to demonstrate through your actions. Likewise, your purpose should not be generic as in "to help other people." All purposes fit under the umbrella of helping others, but what is the particular way in which you will do that? What area of society will you provide for and protect? Will you help youth through coaching; raise funds to cure cancer; serve your community as a member of the school board or town council; or any number of countless causes? I myself have chosen to help married men be great husbands, which is the reason for this very book.

In the timeless movie, *The Dead Poets Society*, Robin Williams who plays Mr. Keating, an English teacher at a boys boarding school, gathers the young men of his classroom closely together in front of the school's trophy case. As the young men stare into the faces of the young men of the distant past, Keating explains why a man reads and writes poetry. He inspires their passion as he eloquently quotes Walt Whitman's poem "Oh Me! Of Life!"

Oh me! Oh life! of the questions of these recurring,
Of the endless trains of the faithless, of cities fill'd with the foolish,
Of myself forever reproaching myself, (for who more foolish than I, and who more faithless?)
Of eyes that vainly crave the light, of the objects mean, of the struggle ever renew'd,
Of the poor results of all, of the plodding and sordid crowds I see around me,
Of the empty and useless years of the rest, with the rest me intertwined,
The question, O me! so sad, recurring—What good amid these, O me, O life?
Answer.
That you are here—that life exists and identity,
That the powerful play goes on, and you may contribute a verse.

As Mr. Keating asks those young men, I ask you:

"What will your verse be?"

Your Character as Revealed by Your Actions

Character, yes, your character. The Oxford English Dictionary defines character as *"the mental and moral qualities distinctive to an individual."* What are the mental and moral qualities that are distinctive to you? Behaviors create habits, habits shape character, and ultimately character governs future behaviors. Character counts: It is your character that defines what you must -- or equally importantly -- must not do. Your character must be explicitly defined and defended with steadfast resolve. When you think of men of character and principles, who are governed by their values, who comes to mind? While most of you will name men of generations long past, one current day example is the late John McCain. He inherited the virtue of honor from the legacy of his father and grandfather and it is their example he spent his life trying to emulate. For him, there was no greater trait than honor and no greater purpose than to make the United States of America a better place for all. And in those rare instances when he compromised his character for personal gain, it pained him to no end. This is not to say his or any other man's behavior is perfect. He made many mistakes along the way, as we all do. It is our character that will bring us back on track at those times when we fall short.

Your character is shaped and molded each day by your actions, particularly in those situations where it is tested. While others influence your character, you are, at the end of the day, the sculptor and sculpture of your character. Take a moment to reflect on your character. What are the characteristics that define who you are, that distinguish you from other men? Make a list that describes your character. Before you begin, you must be 100% objective in your assessment. What do your actions reveal about your character? Are you generous or selfish; aggressive or passive; anxious or patient; brave or cowardly; angry or peaceful; arrogant or humble; hopeful or resigned; honest or deceitful; ambitious or lazy; steadfast or fickle; disciplined or undisciplined?

Be careful, you will be inclined to exaggerate your good qualities and ignore your faults. This is a time to be brutally honest with yourself by asking, "What is the objective evidence in my actions that consistently demonstrates this character trait?" Be hard on yourself and gentle with others.

After you develop your list, ask a few who know you well enough to tell you the truth. Is this list an accurate representation of the man that you are today, and not the man that you aspire to be? Then you need to ask yourself: Do I like what I came up with? Am I satisfied with my character? Does this list detailing your current character represent the man that I aspire to be? For many men, the answer is **no** or at least not in all aspects. Next prepare a list of the character traits that reflect the man that you admire and respect, a man that you would follow. Having done this exercise with hundreds of men, young and old alike, the list is surprisingly consistent. It may look something like this:

Disciplined	Strong	Wise
Generous	Forgiving	Selfless
Courageous	Committed	Purposeful
Playful	Confident	Determined
Compassionate	Humble	Reverent
Passionate	Trustworthy	Caring

Once developed, your list becomes the standard that you must live up to. Any behavior that does not reflect your standard must be eliminated. Men have historically used a "Code of Honor" to define the set of character traits that a man or group of men should aspire to. George Washington was governed by *110 Rules of Civility and Decent Behaviour*, which itself was rooted in a set of rules composed by French Jesuits in 1595.

Benjamin Franklin diligently held himself to his thirteen Virtues. He even developed a daily system scoring his behavior against his chosen virtues. To ensure progress, each week he paid particular attention to one virtue. The first week he focused on temperance. The second week he concentrated his attention on silence, and so on. Using this system, each virtue received intense focus four times per year. What do *you* focus on?

Benjamin Franklin's Thirteen Virtues.

1. TEMPERANCE. Eat not to dullness; drink not to elevation.
2. SILENCE. Speak not but what may benefit others or yourself; avoid trifling conversation.
3. ORDER. Let all your things have their places; let each part of your business have its time.
4. RESOLUTION. Resolve to perform what you ought; perform without fail what you resolve.
5. FRUGALITY. Make no expense but to do good to others or yourself; i.e., waste nothing.
6. INDUSTRY. Lose no time; be always employed in something useful; cut off all unnecessary actions.
7. SINCERITY. Use no hurtful deceit; think innocently and justly, and, if you speak, speak accordingly.
8. JUSTICE. Wrong none by doing injuries, or omitting the benefits that are your duty.
9. MODERATION. Avoid extremes; forbear resenting injuries so much as you think they deserve.
10. CLEANLINESS. Tolerate no uncleanliness in body, cloaths, or habitation.
11. TRANQUILLITY Be not disturbed at trifles, or at accidents common or unavoidable.
12. CHASTITY. Rarely use venery but for health or offspring, never to dulness, weakness, or the injury of your own or another's peace or reputation.
13. HUMILITY. Imitate Jesus and Socrates.

The Boy Scouts govern their conduct with the Scout Law. This begins the hard work of becoming the man you aspire to be, the man who would attract a woman worthy of such a man. Once you define and adopt these behaviors you must conform your conduct to them and in doing so, begin the work of forging your character.

Whom Do You Serve?

Ask yourself: Whom do I serve? What is your response? If you were able to say something other than "Myself", then you are on your path to having a purpose. If you said, "Myself", see what else you might serve. If you naively or worse arrogantly said: "I don't serve anyone," this is not entirely true. If you serve yourself and your personal interests, you are still a boy. The line between being a boy and a man is not about age, it's about the focus on your life. A boy serves himself while a man serves something outside himself: his family, community or purpose. Once you claim a purpose, you will be able to answer this question. Once again, I'll offer a connection to Scouting. In our Scout Oath, a young man promises "to do my duty to God and my country." On the surface it appears harmless enough, until you begin to ask yourself: what is my duty? Merriam Webster defines duty as: obligatory tasks, conduct, service, or functions that arise from one's position. When a scout pays attention to his duty, it will call him forward. We all have a duty.

Then it is time to ask: "How well do I serve?" "Am I obedient to my duty?" There's another challenging word, *obedient,* and then there is its close companion, *obligation*. These are two words that an unbridled ego cannot stand. A man must learn to subordinate his wants to what is required of him -- by the man he declares himself to be.

Circle of Influence and Circle of Control

Now for some this question of purpose and service may be a very challenging one, but it is truly unavoidable. Sooner or later you will have to come to terms with what your life is about. Sooner is certainly better! One way to deal with this is found in Stephen Covey's book, *The Seven Habits of Highly Effective People,* in which he describes three concentric circles.

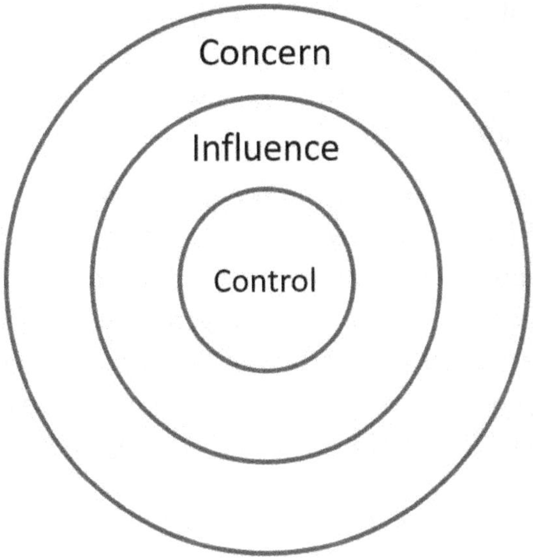

In the outer circle, there are things you may be concerned with but are completely outside of your control, like the weather. If you are affected by such things, you must prepare for them, avoid them if possible, or deal with them if you can't. Huge, worldly issues live out there, like World Hunger. Spending a lot of your energy out there leads to frustration and resignation.

In the middle circle, you have the things that concern you and that you don't control, but that you do have influence on. You should use your influence to improve things in this area. You have influence over your friends, families, or colleagues and you can encourage them to participate with you in some cause or action. While you can't solve World Hunger, you can have an impact on your immediate community. This is the Circle of Influence.

In the center are things you have direct control over, yourself for example, your time, your talents, and your money. You can volunteer your time and donate to an organization or charity that serves something important that you care about. In doing so, you will have a direct impact on your surroundings and begin to serve something outside of yourself. Several positive things will begin to occur. By directing your efforts on the things inside of your control, you can accomplish a lot and as you do, your circle of control and your circle of influence expand.

In relationships you have no control over what other people do, you can only control you own behavior. So, if you find yourself all worked up about what someone else is doing or not doing for that matter, you are only going create greater frustration in yourself. Step back, take stock in your own actions, change them if you need to, and use your actions as means to influence those around you. When coaching men, if they start complaining about their wives' behavior, I remind them that it is 'none of their business', and -- just as when you are driving -- it is best to keep your eyes on the your side of road, lest you start to focus on the other side of the street and wind up crashing. Stay in your lane, master your own behavior and become an example for others to emulate.

Passion, Desire, Ambition, Initiative, and Action

So, the question of your passion is an important one, because passion is the source of ambition and the fuel that drives your initiative. Without this you become passive, weak, or, worse, submissive. A man must have an internal fire that propels him forward. So, it is time to find out what that is for you, wake it up, and feed it!

Passion has several definitions, but one from the Merriam-Webster states: "intense, driving, overmastering feeling or conviction." The depth of your passion is rooted in that which you care for or about. Men who care make sacrifices, big ones. It is care that turns a mercenary into a hero. Care is the central power within you that drives you to deliver on your purpose. What or whom do you care about? Men care deeply and the more you care about something the better care you take of it.

"Those who restrain desire, do so because theirs is weak enough to be restrained; and the restrainer or reason usurps its place & governs the unwilling. And being restrained it by degrees becomes passive till it is only the shadow of desire." William Blake *The Marriage of Heaven and Hell.*

On the other hand, passion leads to initiative and initiative to action. Initiative has become a weak muscle in many men - men who are paralyzed by doubt, doubt in their abilities and therefore doubt in themselves. We have all heard the expression "doubt kills the warrior." Doubt causes you to pause, to question yourself, and in that moment, you are dead, you fail to take action. *"He who hesitates is lost."* You step back instead of stepping forward. How can you develop your initiative, you ask? The answer is: kill the doubt. How do I do that? The answer is simple, but the execution requires an investment of time and effort. Men doubt themselves because they lack confidence. It would be naive to simply suggest: be confident. That's not a sustainable answer.

I have spent two decades leading young men to become leaders through Scouting. To keep them engaged, I remind them of two things. First, that Boy Scouts is *the best experience-based leadership development program there is, bar none*! And second, that

Experience builds skills; Skill builds confidence;
Confidence builds leadership.
First the ability to lead yourself and then to lead others.

A man's confidence is rooted in his ability to trust himself which is based on his skills and abilities. And increasingly men are not having sufficient experiences to develop their self-confidence. So develop yourself through experiences. Begin by helping another man with something he is doing, watch him and learn. With repeated experiences, you will develop that ability and your confidence in yourself will grow. This is the model on which apprenticeships are based. I ask you: can you discipline yourself to take direction from a more experienced man, so that he can help *you* develop?

I believe that men and women are *Designed by God to do Good* and deep down, every man, young and old alike, aspires to be a man that other men can count on. This is true even, if in the moment, they know that they are not. This is not to say that everyone acts in accordance with this design. A life of hardship, abuse, and trauma can lead men to do evil things. However, deep down your conscience, that inner voice of the Holy Spirit, sanctifies you and calls you to do what is right. Recognize that within yourself and let it be something that drives you to action toward good.

Commitment

Commitment is one of the most critically important principles in a man's life and his commitments must be rooted in, and enable, his purpose. Unfortunately, most men are not being taught this by instruction or by seeing it modeled by other men. According to the 2011 US Census bureau, the full-time median income for married men ages 18-64 years old was $55,958, while only $34,634 for single men. That means married man earn 62% more than single men.

So why is that? Are married men somehow smarter? No. Stronger? No! Better in some regard? No.

The married man's competitive advantage
IS his commitment.

Married men make more money because they ***have to***! On the other hand, the single man does not have nearly as many "I have to's" in his life. When life gets hard, it is easier for him to compromise himself saying "I'll do it tomorrow." But we all know, tomorrow never comes.

It is your obligations and responsibilities as a man,
honorably served,
that drive the development of your character!

It doesn't happen any other way. Your obligations and responsibilities help you to become a better man and as a result, you produce better results, which is better for you, your wife, and your family! All of which makes you feel good, further propelling you forward. Furthermore, succeeding at one level prepares you to be successful at the next. It is a never-ending pursuit. When a man knows that others count on him, it pulls him forward, ***past where he quits on his own***, past his doubts and limitations, past his excuses, justifications and lies. This is, has always been, and always will be true!

Your commitments are the actions you do to serve your purpose. For it to be a true commitment, you must allow the commitment to tell you what you must and must not do. If an action will benefit your marriage, for example, you must do it regardless of how you think you feel about it. If an action will cause harm to your marriage, then you must not do it. Period! There is no room for allowing yourself to misbehave. Only take actions that generate positive outcomes and eliminate those that do not. Notice what you say to yourself, just before you do what you know you must. It might sound like: "It's the right thing to do!" Also notice what you say to yourself when you don't do what you know deep down that you must. It might be something like: "I'll do it later" or "I don't care!" The good news is you do know how to serve your commitments; the bad news is you may not do that often enough. So, all there is to do is:

Do what you do well, more often!

If you are a man who has spent the better part of your life avoiding commitments and relating to them as burdens, you have paid dearly for this thinking and you have cheated yourself and those you care about. The solution is to step up and be responsible for something; more importantly, become responsible for someone. Allow the pull of the responsibility, this obligation, to propel you past where you quit on your own, to redefine and refine who you are as a man.

Your marriage and any real commitment that you have is valuable because it requires something of you! It requires the boy to become a man; it requires you to persevere and to strive to be your best. When someone counts on you, it compels you to do your best. Without it, it is not sustainable.

Addiction

There is no shortage of addictions: eating, drugs, smoking, vaping, alcohol, video games, sex, pornography, etc. Ease of access is a contributing factor given the prevalence of every vice; there are few remaining barriers preventing access. And there is recent neuropsychological evidence that reveals how prolonged abuse alters the brain, driving further cravings and making it even more difficult to stop. According to the National Survey on Drug Use and

Health (NSDUH), a staggering 19.7 million American adults, aged 12 and older, battled a substance use disorder in 2017, and this may be understated. Addiction rates are generally higher for men than women. I am not an expert on this topic, but to omit this topic would be careless. For more information, you can find more than 10,000 books on this topic and seek professional help if needed.

Addictions are the opposite of commitments. In fact, they are at war with them and damage your ability to be committed. What I have learned, which may provide you some encouragement and a way to deal with your addictive tendencies, is this: the addiction is the symptom of the problem. It is not the real problem. While this may be controversial, the premise should be considered. The addiction fills a pre-existing void in your soul, a short-term attempt to ease or escape from the pain.

Once addicted, will power alone is rarely enough to keep your addiction at bay. Sure, you can STOP for a period of time, sometimes for a day, maybe a week. But absent something more compelling the addiction will eventually return. Again, pay attention! Notice what you say to yourself just before you engage in your addiction. "I deserve it!", "It doesn't matter", "I'll stop tomorrow" or something similar.

The moment before a man willingly gives in to his addiction, he tells himself a lie!

The most compelling thing that will enable you to stop is to be objective and to recognize the harm that you are causing those that you care about. Only a bigger, more important commitment can ever fill the void and drive out the addiction. Commitments drive out addictions. In Alcoholics Anonymous, this principle is reflected in the essential Twelfth Step as it calls people to "... carry this message to alcoholics ... ." Being invested in others (commitment) through coaching is a powerful way to keep ourselves on the right path and away from our addictions. If you don't have anything or anyone who counts on you, then find something or someone. Seek out something or someone, step up and volunteer to serve. Helping others can help you drive out your addiction.

Doubt and Choice

The archaic definition of doubt is "fear." When you doubt you are in fear of something going wrong, but these are the risks we must take as men in our lives. There are no guarantees in life, no sure things, nothing certain other than death and taxes. Most men are far too familiar with doubt and all too many become paralyzed by it. Doubt is caused by a lack of confidence in your skills and abilities. This is often fueled by your past mistakes or perceived lack of skill which is rooted in your lack of experience. Perhaps you were told that you weren't good enough and took that to heart. Doubt kills our ability to lead ourselves to act when we know that we must. Failing to act when we must only feeds the doubt.

Prolonged doubt can be devastating and leads to hopelessness, which is the gateway to suicide for all too many men. The good news is that doubt can be conquered by: preparation; getting clear instructions and, more importantly, following those instructions; experience and practice; learning from your mistakes or, better yet, learning from others' mistakes; and by asking for help, which men don't like to do as it exposes their doubt. The important thing to note is that these very answers, which are quite good, came from the same men who claimed they wanted to know how to conquer doubt. Interesting. Doubt is really not about not knowing; it's about not acting.

However, the root of all doubt is choice.

It is the thought that you have a choice that creates the doubt!

If you take away the choice there can be no doubt, only action. Now most of you will fervently insist that you have a choice and that you are free to do what you want, when you want; but think again! In order to be the man that you aspire to be, do you really believe that you have a choice? Once you convince yourself that you have a choice, then you will give counsel to your feelings and decide based on whether or not you feel like doing it. You will convince yourself that you don't want to and then justify it with excuses. But this is exactly how you and all men for that matter compromise and sell out that honorable and respected man you aspire to be.

The way to be the man you are called to be is to do what that man requires of you unreservedly!

You may have apprehension or concern about what's to come. That's good, this will keep you alert, but the doubt will fade away. Just imagine yourself living as a man so self-disciplined that you are free of the doubt that holds you back, free from all the justifications that you tell yourself that prevent you from stepping forward powerfully. Wow!

A man's choice is made when he makes a commitment and in doing so gives his word. There was a time when men valued their word and honored their agreements. There was little need for lawyers, because men did what they said they would do. Remember, there is honor in keeping your word. Are you a man who keeps his word? Or do you rescind it when it becomes too hard or when it requires too much, or simply when you "change your mind"? When it comes to your commitments, any time that you don't feel like doing something, know that you must, that there is no choice but to listen to the man who calls you forward. Every decision has already been made by the man that you aspire to be; your job is to keep quiet and do what he tells you to do.

Every Man Likes What He is Good At!

As men, we are ridiculously simple creatures. One thing I have come to realize is that every man, young and old alike, likes what he is good at! Conversely, the things he says he doesn't like are the things that he is not good at. It is a simple manifestation of our competitive spirit. I recall traveling with a car load of Scouts for an overnight camping trip. The boys were playing a game to pass the time when the youngest one who was losing piped out, "I don't like this game!" I counseled the young men about this principle. and they all agreed and they continued playing. Thirty minutes later when the same Scout who was previously losing and was now winning exclaimed, "I like this game!" The same is true about what boys like at school: they like all the classes they are good at and they don't like the subjects where they perform poorly. This becomes a self-fulfilling prophecy as they start investing themselves in the subjects that they "like" and ignoring the ones they don't, which further accentuates their gap in performance.

So, before you buy your own "story" that you are not interested in marriage, begin to learn how to do it well. Speak with men who you believe have good marriages and follow their counsel. Get good at it before you decide that you don't like it. Get really good at it and you could like it a great deal!

In the pages that follow, I will begin to teach you what you need to know, accept, practice, and master so that you can develop the skills, wisdom, and understanding necessary to be really good at marriage. And in doing so, you can enjoy the best fruits of your labors. And who knows, you just might like it!

Ego: The Good and the Bad

Every man has and needs an ego. Your ego can be strong or weak, healthy or unhealthy. A strong and healthy ego is a powerful tool to drive your success without leaving a trail of bodies behind you. It is your ego that causes you to believe that you are great and that you can accomplish something great. You can't succeed without one. A man with a weak ego will be paralyzed with doubt and fail to take the necessary risks to succeed.

Some men compensate for their weak ego by being overly aggressive. You know the type. Their bravado is a fake pretense designed to protect them. A man with a healthy ego does not feel the need to defend himself. Other men try to find themselves in their extravagant cars, fancy clothes and the image they portray. You are not your belongings. You can and should have nice things, but you shouldn't need or be defined by them. Lastly, some men must be the center of attention; they need to feed their egos by what other people think of them. Your identity cannot be based in what other people think of you.

You must cultivate and master your ego.

You should never let anyone else, particularly your wife or a woman you hope to marry, determine your self-worth or hold the key of your self-esteem. No one has that power, unless you willingly give it to them, which you should not. The key to cultivating a healthy ego is to do the work to develop your skills and serve a purpose. In so doing, you will become a man of character that other men can and do count on.

Your Attitude

Your attitude is the lens through which you see your circumstances and every aspect of your life. Your attitude colors ***everything*** you see and influences how you feel. Your attitude governs your perception. Depending on your perception, you can see good in a bad situation and bad in a good situation. The same circumstances viewed through opposing attitudes will yield different outcomes. You alone determine your perception and you are 100% responsible for your attitude. In the movie *Facing the Giants*, Coach Taylor remarks to his team: "Your attitude is the aroma of your heart, if your attitude is not right, your heart is not right." Your ability to master your attitude is the *single* most important determinant of your success. Absent the proper attitude, you will fail to be disciplined and you will convince yourself that it is okay to quit.

So how do you master your attitude? The first step is to pay attention and to use my Attitude Assessment Tool below. It asks you to evaluate your attitude along two dimensions. On the horizontal axis is blame and responsibility. Is it your nature or your mindset to blame others for what is wrong in your life and the world around you? Or are you a man who takes responsibility? Steven Covey is fond of breaking the word responsible into two parts: response and able, yielding "able to respond". When you are able to respond in a manner that leads you and others to the optimal outcome you move to the right.

On the vertical axis is resignation and initiative. Is it your nature or mindset to be resigned to inaction or do you take initiative to have things be different? By combining the two dimensions, the matrix provides four quadrants. The Quitter is resigned that nothing will change and that he can't do anything about it, all the while blaming others. This man is irrelevant. The Disruptor takes initiative, but while still blaming others, his actions disrupt others' efforts to make positive change. Moving along the bottom horizontal, some men are characterized by the Procrastinator. They recognize that they are responsible. But these men lack the discipline that enables them to act decisively, so nothing changes. The ideal attitude is that of the Servant Leader. This man believes he is responsible and takes initiative. Those in the middle are just Along for the Ride. These men are lukewarm, complacent, waiting for other men to lead them.

Attitude Assessment Tool

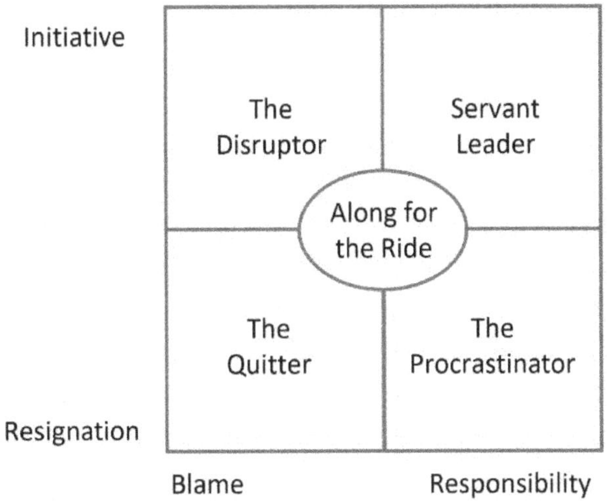

While men spend some time in each quadrant, you need to assess where you spend most of your time. What brings me hope is that in all my interactions with men, young and old, in Scouting and outside, the men aspire to be a Servant Leader. It is a powerful internal force in a man's life. The challenge is living up to that intention.

Now the real power comes from keeping track of how much time you spend in each quadrant. And men are so competitive that we will alter our behavior to manipulate our score. At the end of the day record the percentage of time you spent that day in each category. If you do this and actually use the Attitude Assessment

Tool, over time you will gradually move up and to the right. Benjamin Franklin understood the power of keeping score using his own system to measure himself against the thirteen virtues he valued in order to develop his character.

I gave this to one young man who was going back to college after a year hiatus and two weeks later when I asked him how it was going, he reluctantly responded "The damn thing is working." Oaths, motivational videos, inspiring quotes, and role models are powerful aids that can shape and mold your attitude. Find one that works for you and use it every day.

Self-Discipline

After mastering your attitude, self-discipline is the second most important quality that you must develop. This is your ability to do what you *know* you *need* to do, *when* you need to do it, regardless of how you *feel* about it. Your job is to do your job, when your job needs to be done, in the way your job needs to be done, to the best of your ability. Self-discipline is the one quality that conquers procrastination, doubt, and any other form of excuse. It must be a core quality of your character as a man and it reflects your ability to be in control of and master yourself. With self-discipline, doing what is right becomes a habit, a deliberate way of being, instead of an occasional happy accident.

You should think of self-discipline as a muscle. Just like any other muscle, if you exercise it, it will get stronger. If you don't exercise it, it will atrophy. You can develop this muscle through seemingly simple activities. I have challenged my scouts to begin each day by saying the Scout Oath. The Scout Oath is a promise that a scout makes to himself and serves to hold him up to a higher standard in his life.

> "On my honor I will do my best to do my duty to God and my Country and to obey the Scout Law; to help other people at all times; to keep myself physically strong, mentally awake, and morally straight."

While it only takes 15 seconds to say, surprisingly those young men who have accepted this challenge have reported remarkable results. One young man commented boldly, "It makes my life go smoothly." Equally apparent is how quickly the positive results disappear when a young man discontinues this daily routine. Many, having had the experience on their own, have committed to using this for the rest of their lives, as have I. And, you don't need to have been a Scout to say the Scout Oath and have it work its magic for you.

Engaging in a ***daily*** practice or discipline is the best way to become disciplined. Admiral William H. McRaven wrote *Make Your Bed: 10 Life Lessons from a Navy SEAL* where he describes the power in being disciplined. Nearly anything can become a discipline. Any specific activity that you do for a specific frequency, time, and duration may qualify. It is important to be specific so it is clear that you did or didn't do it. Your daily discipline demonstrates that you can keep your word. It is also the best way to identify and begin to overcome the excuses you use to keep you from doing the important and challenging things in your life.

Master Craftsman

As you embark on your career and your life's purpose, challenge yourself to be the best at everything that you do. In the current era of "everybody gets a trophy", our society has devalued the recognition of hard work and the development of one's skills. Resist the temptation to dilute your definition of success down to your level of performance. Instead, commit yourself to be the one that others seek out in your trade or profession.

The performance of your skills must exceed the opinion of your skills!

While some may be particularly gifted, everybody has the ability to be great at what they do. Yet few dedicate themselves to the effort required to become a skilled craftsman. While seemingly more relevant in the trades, the concept of being a craftsman can be applied to any skill or profession.

Several years ago, I saw a bumper sticker on a tradesman truck that read, "100 years from now, they will marvel at my work. None will know my name." This epitomizes the character of a craftsman, highly skilled with his ego in check. Don't let your good works go to your head and don't settle for good enough. Good enough is never really good enough.

King, Magician, Lover, Warrior

In your quest to clearly define yourself as a man, another useful lens through which to look at yourself is the four archetypes detailed by Douglas Gillette and Robert Moore in their book: *King, Magician, Lover, Warrior*. They advocate that these four archetypes are timeless and that every man reflects some qualities of each, in different proportions perhaps. Think of the imagery embodied in each.

The benevolent King, not a dictator, is charged with providing for and protecting everything and, more importantly, everyone in his kingdom. A king must lead with influence and only resort to authority when absolutely necessary. Yes, he has the authority, but with that comes the responsibility to know how and when to use it.

The Magician understands how things work and directs present actions in order to manifest the desired future. What must I do today, to create the life and the future that I desire? He understands that all actions have consequences; it is unavoidable. A man who denies and ignores the consequences of his actions will suffer along with those around him.

The Lover as you would expect has roots in the arts and the wonder, pleasure, joy and richness of life. A man should enjoy the fruits of his life, just not allow himself to be consumed by them.

The Warrior sacrifices and serves his kingdom. He is a man of honor and knows what he is living for, as he knows what he is willing to die for. Absent a kingdom to serve, the Warrior becomes a mercenary.

These four dimensions provide a man stability, equipping him with ability to draw on the necessary qualities as the situation requires. There is strong interdependence among the archetypes. The Lover balances the Warrior who serves the King who is guided by the Magician. Even the King must submit to the council of the Magician. Think of the interplay between King Arthur and Merlin in the Knights of the Round Table. It is important that you develop all aspects and that you surround yourself with men who are strong in areas where you are not. Gillette and Moore's book is also quite helpful as it explores the under and over developed aspects of each archetype, which is very useful if you are a father of sons.

Emotions vs. Being Emotional

As mentioned earlier, men care deeply and it is important to be motivated by that care. Men feel grief, sorrow, joy, and anger. We will explore anger further in Chapter Five. Men do have emotions. However, a man should never become emotional or make decisions based on his emotions.

Advances in neuroscience and behavior by Professor Emeritus Richard Haier at the University of California, Irvine and Rex Jung from the University of New Mexico and subsequent studies reveal that men's and women's brains are different at a neurological and molecular level. "The structural roots of intelligence may differ by gender. In women higher IQ scores are associated with more gray and white matter in frontal language areas, whereas in men higher IQ correlates with more gray matter in posterior sensory integration areas." (Haier, Nov/Dec 2009). Their study reveals in part that men have nearly 6.5 times the amount of gray matter related to general intelligence compared with women, whereas women have nearly ten times the amount of white matter related to intelligence compared to men. In overly simplified terms, the gray matter is for processing and the white matter for wiring the processing centers together.

Women's brains appear to be designed for language, intuition, and emotion, while men's brains appear to be designed for logic, singular focus, and action. These are fundamental structural differences. It is hard to argue based on basic observation of young and old alike. Perhaps the few men who got emotional were eaten by the saber tooth tiger!

Men should never make decisions based solely on their emotions. Why not? Because your emotions are fickle, they change. Your emotions can vary wildly based on your attitude at that moment, your situation, or worse what you claim as your "feelings". I am sure that you have heard other men say and perhaps you yourself may have said "I don't feel like it!" as a legitimate reason not to do something that you know you should do. Such statements of feelings are nothing more than a well-crafted excuse. A man who is emotional allows his emotions to dictate his behavior; he is out of control because his emotions are in control of him.

An emotional man can't be counted on or trusted.

Because he will behave differently depending on how he feels in the moment.

It is very important to pay attention to your true emotions; they provide important insight. However, you must vet them over time and against your attitude and responsibilities. A man who has no emotions is numb and a man who is numb is dangerous. This is often a result of severe trauma in a man's life. While in the middle of the trauma, the best response is to suppress your emotions so you can act. However, if a man fails to deal with his emotions, he may remain numb long after the experience is over. This can be dangerous because it distances him from what he cares about.

Be careful not to place too much importance on "being happy", as it is the least important thing. Besides, who decides if you are happy? You do of course! This means that you can change your mind. You can do something one day and be happy, and do the very same thing another day and decide that you are not. "Happy" is more of an attitude than a feeling or emotion. Happiness is like eating a piece of chocolate cake or candy: it pleases you in a moment, but then it's gone and leaves you wanting more for yourself. Fulfillment that comes from serving your purpose is like eating steak: it nourishes and strengthens you. A man should seek to be fulfilled by doing something that makes his life count. No man wants on his gravestone, "At least he was happy." So, if you have convinced yourself that you are not happy, then change your mind. That's right! Don't insist on torturing yourself by exaggerating the difficulties in your life. If you can do this when life is relatively easy, then when life really throws you a challenge, you can maintain your attitude and work through whatever needs your attention.

Bring Yourself into the Light

For anyone who's spent anytime painting, you are well aware that as you bring more and brighter light to bear on the wall, the more and smaller the imperfections you find. You also know how easy it is to accept less than your best when you think that you are alone, by yourself where no one is watching. Darkness hides and light reveals. As you progress through this rest of the chapters, be aware and pay attention. Allow this text to bring to light any aspects of yourself or your character that you wish to develop. As yourself if you would admire a man who lived his life the way that you are living yours? If yes, hopefully this book will inspire you with the courage and conviction to double down and continue. If the answer is no, simply asking the question may compel you to change for the better. Consider reading this book with another man and share your observations and actions with him. At the end of the day, you are in charge.

Closing the Gap

Men don't like change and we don't like to change. However, for most of us there is a gap between the man that we are now and the man that we aspire to be. If you are to live your life as the man that you admire and respect, then you have to change for the better. Thus, begins the hard work of cultivating your character.

Closing the gap requires five things: first that you identify the change; second that you establish a daily discipline; third that you link it to something bigger than yourself; fourth that you establish a system of accountability; and finally, that you are ***willing*** to change. The last point is often the hardest. Your ability to change is not rooted in knowing how to change, it is rooted in your willingness to change.

Identifying the change is the easy part. You can find the root of the change by identifying a current behavior that does not reflect the character of the man you admire from earlier in this chapter. Does a disciplined man arrive late to work? Does a generous man withhold his care? Does an honest man cheat? Does a committed man give into his addictions or quit on his family?

Then comes the more challenging part, effecting and sustaining the change. You know from your own experience that it is nearly impossible to effect real change on your own. Absent the courage of another man who will tell you the cold hard objective truth, you will dismiss the need to change and believe your own excuses and justifications about the impact of your behavior.

To be effective, the change must be focused on what you will do, not what you won't do. Instead of losing weight, focus on eating healthy. Instead of stopping smoking, commit yourself to exercise. The daily practice of preparing your food or running 2 miles a day will lead your forward and create new habits that support the change in your character.

The only thing that compels a man to change is when he clearly sees that his actions are compromising what he says he is committed to.

If you are struggling to lose weight, to exercise regularly, to stop smoking, or to become disciplined, it is likely because you are doing it for yourself. Because it is a good idea. That alone is not enough. It is dangerously easy to quit on yourself. However, if you connect your change to something bigger, to something that is important, then you create the necessary tug that will pull you past where you quit on your own. It is critical that you link your change to something that you are committed to. If you accept that the people that are counting on you are waiting for you to change, then it becomes easier to follow through. You may not be able to stop smoking for yourself, but you may be willing for your family.

Another powerful tool is accountability. When you establish a system of accountability with another man to whom you are required to justify and explain your actions or decision, then you are more likely to follow through. It is important that you choose a man that you respect so that you won't let him down by not doing what you said you were going to do.

Connecting the change to something bigger than yourself and the system of accountability are the two cornerstones that will fuel your willingness to change. If you apply these five steps, then you can accomplish anything.

Key Thoughts

- If you don't know where you are going, then any road will do.
- Experience builds skills; skills build confidence; and confidence builds leadership.
- It is your responsibilities and obligations as a man, honorably served that drive the development of your character.
- You are *Designed by God to do Good*!
- Your character is revealed by the sacrifices you will and will not make.
- The moment before a man willingly gives into his addiction, he tells himself a lie.
- An emotional man can't be counted on or trusted.
- The performance of your skills must exceed the opinion of your skills.

Recommended Actions

- Choose your purpose.
- Master your attitude.
- Engage in a daily discipline.
- Become a craftsman. Commit yourself to mastering your trade.
- Do what you do well more often.
- Do what is required of you, unreservedly!

Questions for Reflection

1. What is your purpose? What do you stand for? What is your time on this planet really about? What are you willing to die for?

2. What is your default attitude? What is the attitude you must develop to be your best?

3. What kind of man do you seek to be? Make a list of the qualities of character you aspire to have and must develop within yourself.

4. What must you change about your character and what daily discipline will you engage in?

Chapter Two – Getting Ready

"Proper prior planning prevents
piss poor performance."
My Father

Compatibility

Compatibility is an essential ingredient for a healthy marriage. Compatible: *"capable of existing together in harmony."*[3] What a fabulous definition. The single greatest element of compatibility is your values and beliefs, *including* your faith, which unfortunately all too many of you have ignored and neglected. Just because you are attracted to her physically and you have similar interests, it doesn't guarantee that you are compatible. True compatibility runs much deeper than that: it is personal as it is based on your shared values.

Two things are of great importance when entering a serious relationship with a woman. First, you must be clear about your values. Second you must be objective in your assessment of her values so you can gauge how compatible you are before things go too far. Let's take a deeper look at values.

Values Matter

Shared values form the foundation of your relationship and your marriage. Not being clear about *your* values or, equally damaging, compromising your values in order to *'get the girl'* leads to almost certain failure, without great work and compromise by both parties.

The Oxford Dictionary defines values as "your principles or standards of behavior, one's judgment of what is important in life." You can think of them as your own personal 'Code of Conduct'. In today's popular 'do it if it feels good' society, it is increasingly

---

[3] Oxford English Dictionary

challenging to uphold your own standards. Having a wife with compatible values, beliefs, and behaviors will strengthen your ability to stay focused on what is important to you in your life. A like-minded woman will encourage you, not criticize you for what you stand for. A good woman will also let you know when you fall short of them. Marrying a like-minded woman will eliminate a whole host of conflicts that would otherwise emerge once you have children.

Faith Matters

As the foundation for values, faith matters most. A man's faith provides him an external compass for his life. Without an external compass, a man will be led astray by his own unreliable internal compass, guided by his own temperamental desires, or worse, by his feelings. Increasingly, many men dismiss the role that faith serves in their lives, leaving them unprepared during times of need, and overly confident in times of prosperity. Your faith provides you counsel and community. It will guide the direction of your life and provide a foundation for your marriage and family.

In marriage, I have seen all too many couples struggle to stay together when they don't share the same faith. In some cases, the couple have explicitly different faiths: the man is Christian, and the woman is Jewish or vice versa. Increasingly marriages are void of faith altogether because the couple is consumed by other activities and they don't see the value of faith. More often than not, it is the man who has not claimed -- or worse, has rejected -- his faith.

While you are dating you can easily and naively persuade yourself that faith doesn't matter. You spend "equal time" with each other's extended family and religious customs if you have them. For the single man, this is easy as he likes what he is getting from this new girl. When you get married, it starts to become a little awkward. Over time you begin to subordinate your preferences to hers. Being controlled by her approval, you compromise and give in. It often happens so slowly that you dismiss it as insignificant at the time. But you end up like a frog in a pot of water that is gradually heated: it doesn't wake up until it is too late and gets cooked. Once you have children, your faith becomes more important and it gets more complicated.

Like it or not, you are called to be the spiritual leader of your family. The research is clear, the primary determinant that a family will attend church is if the ***father*** does. "It is the religious practice of the father of the family that, above all, determines the future attendance at or absence from church of the children."[4] Invest some time and effort to actively discern for yourself the role faith will play in your life. But don't dismiss it out of hand.

Money Matters

Just behind faith, money matters next because ***your*** relationship with money is the ***best*** reflection of who you are. "For where your treasure is, there your heart will be also."[5] What is your relationship with money? How much do you make and how much are you willing to earn? How much do you spend? Most importantly, on what and on whom you spend your money reveals the TRUTH about your values. Do your actions reveal that you are a generous man or do they reveal something else?

---

[4] The Demographic Characteristics of National Minorities in Certain European States, edited by Werner Haug and others, published by the Council of Europe Directorate General III, Social Cohesion, Strasbourg, January 2000.

[5] Matthew 6.21

***If you are selfish with your money,
you will be selfish in your marriage.***

Marriage is not about what you get from it, it is about what you have to give to it! You ***must*** learn to be generous and to make sacrifices, not as a burden, but as an expression of the man that you intend to be. You must also develop the will power and self-control with your money that are required in order to make the needed investments in your future. Walter Mischel, the creator and author of *The Marshmallow Test*, demonstrates the critical importance of self-control in predicting the quality of someone's life. Your money is your marshmallow.

Since money is one of the most frequently cited causes of conflict, having compatible views with regard to finances is one of the most important cornerstones of a healthy marriage. If you and your wife don't share the same discipline around money, it will be a constant source of friction in your marriage. A woman should never marry a man who is undisciplined with his money and neither party wishes to inherit the large debt of another. Ultimately, you need to be responsible for your finances, so, now is a good time to gain some discipline around it.

Your Career

A man's career is his way of caring for his family, of being the provider for his wife and children. Contrary to popular belief, having a career is ***not*** a privilege that men have and women have been somehow denied by an evil patriarchal society. A man's career is his obligation; it is the essential way for him to provide for his family. Think about it, there is a reason that we call it "WORK"! Having children is a God-given privilege that only women are blessed with and men are not. Why a woman would prioritize her job over being a mother is confusing to me. This is not to say that I don't think women should work. Many need to. But it's about her priorities. What is most important, her children or her career? If her career is more important, then she will be forced to compromise her role as a mother in order to advance her career. And your children will pay the consequences for it. They can't be equal. In the time of need who wins out? There is *plenty* of time, once the children have grown, for your wife to have a career, if she still believes that she has to have one. By then most women, given the choice, would change their minds and appreciate the gift they were given by their husbands.

As more and more women begin to think that they have to have a career, this subject gets more challenging, but it should never be ignored. If you both have a career, is she willing to put your career ahead of hers? It is far too costly to a man for him to subordinate his career to his wife's career. One of my favorite sayings is: "Just because you can, doesn't mean that you should!" Yes, you could subordinate your career and become the "Mr. Mom," but *should* you? What are the consequences to you, to your wife, and to your children? Be honest with yourself. Most men are not equipped to be good mothers. That is what your children need, the nurturing love of a good mother. You should focus on being a good father. A recent study by the Council on Contemporary Families found that: "a woman's job has little impact on the strength of a marriage, but her husband's employment status can be a threat."

Equally destructive, a growing number of men expect that their wives will work. They look at her income as a source of "easy" money. It becomes about what she can contribute to him, rather than what he will provide to her. Do not expect her to do your job.

It is best if a man is willing to be 100% responsible for the financial well-being of his family and that he leads them to live within their means.

This responsibility will pull you forward, and it will make you a better man. More on this in a moment.

While opinions on this topic have changed, it isn't clear they've changed for the better. Society has identified some of the benefits, but has ignored most of the negative consequences of this trend, particularly on boys. They use logic that ignores the natural gifts and abilities of women that make them better equipped to care for and nurture young children. Sure, a man can do a reasonably good job, but is good, good enough? Is it good enough for your children?

My wife and I got married young according to today's prevailing standards, and she worked for many years before we were able to have her stay home to be a full-time mother. So after six years of working, we could finally afford to have Nancy stay home full-time with our children. Although we often talked about it, it wasn't real until Nancy was about to submit her resignation letter.

What happened next, Nancy and I weren't prepared for. For her part, Nancy had to trust, unconditionally, that I would care for her for the rest of her life - a ***giant*** leap of faith for a woman to make in light of today's divorce rates. On my side, I had to accept that responsibility.

Prior to that moment, I wasn't really 100% responsible for my family's financial needs and now I was. I had to step up; I had to be better, to become more disciplined, to work harder. To this day, we remember how our marriage almost instantly grew stronger; the deeper trust yielded greater intimacy in that very moment. We were no longer two halves each sharing in our portion of the work. We were now ***completely interdependent*** and we could each focus our energies on what we do best. Nancy could now focus on caring for the family and I could focus on the honorable task of providing for them. This has been the greatest gift I could give to my children. I use the analogy of a bus. The man should drive the bus and the woman should care for everyone inside the bus. Leadership and caring working in harmony.

Early on, Nancy felt dismissed by other career-minded women because she was a full-time mom. I assured her that there isn't a woman on the planet who, deep down, didn't want what she has: a man who loves and cares for her, and the privilege to care for her children. More than twenty-five years later, she knows this is true and she thanks me for giving her that blessed opportunity.

Which came first, the chicken or the egg? Was I successful and that allowed me to provide for my family, or was it the responsibility to my family that required that I become successful? While the former is true, the latter is the truth. Do your children deserve a full-time mother? There is no shortage of research suggesting that this is best for them.

Children and Family

It is essential for you and your wife to be on the same page regarding children. Today, many men and women think that they don't want children. This is often driven by an "avoidance of responsibility" or a doubt in their ability to be parents. When thinking about children, it is easy to see the things that you enjoy that you will likely need to give up. There are real sacrifices for you to make. And not being a father, you have little experiential evidence of the benefits that would encourage you to make those sacrifices. As with marriage, becoming a father is an important rite of passage in your life. Once a father, you will always be a father and it will change your life forever and for the better!

Children are permanent. But they also transform a couple into a family, something greater than two individuals focused on their own needs. There is a shared responsibility that binds you to your wife, if you are willing.

If she wants children and you don't (more on this later), the honorable thing to do is to let her go so that she can enjoy the blessings of children. Likewise, if you know you want children and she doesn't (more on this later), then you should also let her go. *You will pay a high price, if you abandon your desire to have children for this woman.*

First you must get clear for yourself: Is a family, having children, part of your legacy? Then you must find a woman whose values align with yours. Do this early in your courtship so you do not to waste her time.

Giving and Taking

It is generally true for men, when they are dating, that the relationship is based more on what the man wants to take (or get) from the woman than what he has to give her. In order to be ready for marriage, you must have moved past your focus on taking (receiving) and be prepared to give even if and especially when you don't receive anything in return. Giving to get something in return is not giving, it is trading and manipulation. When you don't get what you want in return, do you stop giving and then blame the other person? A boy serves himself taking what he wants. A man serves something outside of himself. This is a defining line between being a boy and becoming a man, and the world is full of boys masquerading as men.

Sex

Men trade intimacy for sex and women trade sex for intimacy.

It is a dangerous game that men and women play. As a man, you may think this is an even exchange, but it is not and the consequences are very real. Women pay a high emotional price. More on this in Chapter Seven. Furthermore, neither the quality nor the quantity of sex is a suitable basis for a life-long relationship.

Mark Gruber, in the third segment of his series on "Laugh Your Way to a Better Marriage", presents an outstanding segment on sex and the forces at work in a relationship. In a pre-marital mindset, if you are honest with yourself, sex is about you taking something from a woman. As you approach marriage, sex becomes about giving and not taking: giving your wife your time, intimacy, and connection. It becomes much more about what you have to give as a man, your desire for intimacy and taking care of your wife. It moves beyond your physical desire for what is she going to do for you or what you are going to take from her. You begin to become honorable.

Unfortunately, sex is often the easiest way for a woman to control a man. Equally unfortunate, far too many women suffer from low self-esteem. Lacking self-confidence, they don't know any other way to attract and keep a man other than through sex. And since women know other women will resort to using sex to get a man and now men expect it, many women who may prefer to wait feel compelled to have sex to get their man. This behavior is exploited by ABC's popular show *The Bachelor,* where 20 women compete to get a single man. This reality is a sad commentary on the state of the relationships between men and women.

The average man likewise is so lazy that once he gets sex from one woman, he isn't willing to do the work that got it for him in the first place. He starts to expect it and when he doesn't get it, he blames her instead of taking responsibility for being a man that a woman would want to be with. You are not ready to be married if you still have a pre-marital mindset and are consumed, or worse, controlled by your need for sex. It is good for a man to spend time alone, at least a year, by himself so he can be comfortable by and with himself. Until you can be with yourself, you are not prepared to be with someone else.

Intimacy and Bonding

Separate from sex, and more important, is intimacy. Intimacy for men and women are quite different. A man's biological sex drive to procreate leads him to have sex with many women, because until recent advances in DNA testing, he could never be certain that a child was of his own seed. On the other hand, when a woman is pregnant, there is no doubt that the child is her own. And being pregnant and vulnerable, a woman's need for the security provided by her mate to ensure that her child is safe from harm compels her to keep one man around. Intimacy or bonding for a man occurs immediately after orgasm. A man's body releases oxytocin during kissing, hugging, and most significantly after ejaculation. The biological design for the benefit of the child and the survival of the species is that the man will become bonded to the mother and stick around to provide for and protect the mother and the child. The more intimate moments you share with your wife, the higher the oxytocin level you will enjoy.

Conversely, if you have sex with many women, your ability to pair-bond with your future wife will be diminished; the more conquests you have the harder pair-bonding will become. The experiences and erotic images will be burned into your memory forever. There are always consequences.

Women also suffer social and emotional consequences. While a man may want to date and have sex with a woman who's had multiple partners, he is much less likely to want to marry one. Also, the probability that a woman will get married declines steadily as she ages. The popularity of dating apps such as Tinder, where a woman's photo can determine if she is "swiped right" or chosen by a man unduly inflates the importance of physical beauty over quality of her character. This further erodes a woman's self-esteem as she competes in an increasingly sex-oriented culture.

Love is a Verb

Contrary to popular belief, love is not an independent emotion but a biological response to an action, namely *yours*. All too often, what a man mistakes for love is infatuation - the thrill of the pursuit which quickly fades once the pursuit is over. The most valuable definition for love that I know is:

Love is giving WITHOUT expectations.

Are you able to care for your wife without expecting something in return? If you are honest with yourself, you will admit that much of your giving during dating came with many very real expectations! It is your expectations of others that are the source of the disappointment in your life. Are you secure enough in yourself as a man that you can care for your wife without expecting anything in return? Your expectations of her also rob your wife of the joy of giving herself to you. The only expectations you should have are those you have of yourself.

A successful man, a man serving his purpose, must be able to give, give, and give some more, to be generous, absent the ugly expectations of getting something in return. You must be able to focus on "what do I have to give to this relationship" rather than "what will I take from this relationship."

If you think you need something from the relationship, then you are not ready to be in one.

How well you do is a true reflection of who you are, as your character is revealed by the sacrifices you make. What kind of man do you seek to be?

How does She Control You?

Every woman needs a man that she can't control; the only way she can know if she can control you is to try!

If she can control you, then you are of no value to her! If you allow a woman to control you, then you are not prepared to be married. Before you consider spending your life with a woman, you must learn to live without a woman and to not need them. If there is anything that you think you need from a woman, you will compromise yourself to get it, and in so doing allow it to control you.

If you are controlled by a woman's attention, affection, sex, approval, or money, then you will fail to be the man that you must be in your marriage.

When challenged on something important, you will give in and succumb to your need for her acceptance and approval of you.

"How can I tell if I am being controlled by her?" you ask. If you alter your behavior in order to get something from her or to avoid her disapproval, then you are being controlled. You have allowed yourself to be controlled by something that you think you need that you think she has. While many men are consumed by sex (read as "controlled"), increasingly men are controlled by their need for a woman's approval. When a man is insecure with himself, he needs his woman's approval. For her approval, he will compromise himself and do unusual and unnatural things to win her acceptance. If you lack that level of trust in yourself, you will change the way you dress, what you eat, where you go; what you say or how you say it, or even who your friends are. It would be quite funny if it wasn't so painfully true. So, pay attention!

If you are changing your external behavior to win her acceptance, then you are being controlled. *If she can control you, she will.* Worse, if she can control you, then other women will be able to control you, which puts her relationship with you at risk. If she can control you, you are failing. If she can control you, then you are of no use to her. She is worse off with you than without you and *she will get rid of you before she gets hurt.*

This is by no means to say that you shouldn't do things for your wife. You should. But you should do it because it is the right thing to do, not in order to get anything in return. You should enjoy, appreciate, and care for your wife. However, you will not be able to sustain this if you are being controlled by something you think she has that you think you need. When she stops giving it to you, you will stop being generous with her if you aren't getting what you think you need in return.

I believe this recent need for a woman's approval is the consequence of *men not spending enough time with other men* and spending too much time with women. The paradox at play here is: the less you need, the more you get. No woman will give her approval to a man who needs it. And if you don't need it, she will give you plenty of it.

Earn the Respect of Other Men

Men are naturally wired by and value the respect of other men. Unfortunately, you must compete in this powerful game of life with and against other men in order to earn it. You must step forward, take risks, and lead yourself and others forward in honorable pursuits for the common good. This may sound trite, but it is unmistakably true. Remember George Washington states, "Human happiness and moral duty are inseparably linked."

Absent the respect of other men, absent strong masculine, trusting relationships, men frequently don't trust themselves. Men try to fill this void by seeking the approval and acceptance of women. The approval of women is a cheap substitute for what really fuels a man's spirit: the respect of other men. Furthermore, if you need a woman's approval, she will ***never*** give it to you! Didn't you ever wonder why the 'good girls' are attracted to the 'bad boys'? It is not that they secretly want to be bad, it's because the 'bad' boys aren't controlled by others, and rightly or wrongly have the respect of others and therefore provide the girl security.

Instead of chasing the approval of women, engage in honorable acts of service with other men. What a woman truly desires is an honorable man who is respected by other honorable men, men of courage, conviction, discipline, purpose, initiative: a man with a strong generous spirit. Become one and your need for approval will fade, leaving you free to appreciate her acceptance when it comes.

Armed with the respect of other men, you will be self-confident, powerful, and have something to give your woman, give those you care about, and give your community. You will become a man that your wife can rely on, not a boy that she needs to mother and take care of.

Develop Strong Masculine Relationships

Life is challenging and even more difficult when you try to navigate the storms of life on your own. I am certain that you are all keenly aware of your own doubts and the uncertainty inherent in the risks that you must take in your life. Left unchecked, these doubts can stop you dead in your tracks. A small circle of men of high character can provide you confidence just as a life-jacket does when navigating treacherous waters. Even if you don't actually use it, knowing that you have it can keep the fear and doubt at bay. And when you do need it, your small team will propel you forward and have your back if needed.

Men who develop trusting relationships with other men have a competitive advantage over men who don't. Men you trust can counsel you in all matters of life; provide a different perspective when considering options; compensate for skills or knowledge that you lack, and create connections to others in their network. It is critically important that you cultivate your personal network of allies. It will keep you from making costly mistakes, inspire you to action, and open up countless doors to opportunities you would have never seen.

Your ability to develop trusting relationships with other men will be strongly influenced, either good or bad, by the quality of relationship that you have with your father. If you have learned to respect your father it will be easier to respect other men. If you have a strained or damaged connection with your father, it will likely hinder your willingness to trust other men.

Prepare Yourself

The first step to developing an attitude of learning is to accept how little you know. As you are maturing into manhood, you must also prepare yourself by learning how to be in relationship with a woman. This is NOT a natural ability. It is a skill that you must learn, develop, practice, and master. Failure to do so will put you on a path to failure. Thinking that you already know will cause you to become overconfident and may lead to your demise and the demise of your relationships.

Since most men, and women for that matter, enter marriage ill - prepared, no one should be surprised with how many marriages fail. A man should learn how to be in a relationship with a woman with the same effort that he exerts for learning anything else that is important in his life. To be prepared, a man must develop wisdom and skill, and he should be trained by counsel and through experience. Finding an experienced man, who has demonstrated his proficiency in his marriage, to mentor you can be invaluable. However, you must actually do what he tells you to do. If you second-guess him, you are leaning on your own understanding and wishful thinking, the consequences of which are disastrous.

Likewise, short relationships, three months or less, with different women provide an opportunity for you to see how ***you*** behave in a relationship. How do you respond to the responsibilities that accompany the benefits of being in that relationship? *Can you end a relationship that you know isn't a good fit for you or for her? Most men can't.* Again, you must pay attention and be objective. It takes initiative and investment to begin a new relationship and self-confidence to expose yourself to the probability of rejection. You may experience a sense of loss at the end of a relationship. Notice if your sense of identity or status is based on whom you are dating. These 'practice relationships' will provide valuable experience, perspective, and understanding of yourself and of women. Without this you will mistakenly think that you know what you are doing and that your woman is somehow unique and different from the others.

Being prepared requires your commitment. This is more than just experience; it requires an intentional investment of time to develop an understanding of the important dynamics and differences between men and women. This is one area where ignorance is not bliss and can lead to very costly consequences for you, for her, and for your family.

Depression and Suicide

I am not a psychologist, so if you or a friend are struggling with depression or thoughts of suicide then seek professional counsel immediately. This is a complicated and challenging subject. There are different contributing factors at various stages in a man's life. According to the CDC, in 2017 there were 47,173 suicides in the US and it is the second leading cause of death for young adults aged 15-34, and the rates are highest in middle age—white men in particular.

Following the market collapse in the early 2000's, the suicide rate in men spiked dramatically, mostly older men who lost their jobs and could no longer provide for their families. As a man our self-worth is closely tied to our ability to provide for those we care about and when we fail at that it is devastating. Men who have experienced great loss or are alone are also susceptible.

On the other end are young men, who have lost hope for their future. Paralyzed by doubt and their own insecurities, they begin to question the value and meaning of their lives. Suicide rates of male US veterans are alarming. Young men trained for combat, who served our country, return with no place or sense of belonging. The very thing they are good at has no place in our civilized society and the trauma of war is an ever-present ghost in their lives.

Recently a man close to me committed suicide. He was an older gentleman who had enjoyed much success in his life. He was a husband, father, and grandfather, someone whom you would least expect. Regrettably, his health had been failing and he was in pain, and as a result began to struggle with depression. From the outside he had so much to live for, but his physical inability to do what he loved fueled his depression. If you're suffering, don't keep it to yourself! Pay attention to the men around you and get help if you need it.

Masculine Leadership

Be careful, the life you lead may be your own.

Leadership: "the power or ability to lead others." Consider that leadership is 50% about leading yourself. You must have sufficient self-discipline to lead yourself and be in control of yourself ... at all times. If you are not, you are OUT OF CONTROL, and when you are out of control, you are Dangerous!

I advocate the ideal definition of masculine leadership in the following statement:

The measure of a man is his willingness to be responsible for that which he is not responsible for!

As the man of the house, you set the tone and are 100% responsible for that. You set and uphold the standards not by your rules, but by your responsibilities. You should apply the well-known fundamental principle of leadership: If things are going well, your wife gets the credit. If things are not going well, you take the responsibility. Always. Period. That's your job, get over it!

Worse yet, if your masculine presence is weak, you will be attracted to an overly masculine woman to compensate for your own shortcomings and your marriage and children will suffer for it. Remember, you are ALWAYS leading; the challenge is to be responsible for the quality of that leadership. If you have any question regarding the quality of your leadership as revealed by your actions, all you need to do is to ask yourself:

"How would things be if everyone was doing what I am doing?"

You must be objective and if you don't like the answer you must change your attitude, your character, and your actions.

But how does a man develop leadership? Where does it come from? Your ability to lead is rooted in your confidence. Absent confidence, your doubt will cripple your initiative and you will fail to act when called upon. Your confidence in turn rests on your skills and abilities which grow from your experiences in life. Absent the experience, it all falls apart. The opposite is likewise true. The greater your experiences, in frequency, scope, and scale, the greater your skills. This will fuel your confidence, which will conquer your doubt and compel you to take initiative to lead yourself and others. A man who is confident and secure can lead. A man who is not confident will be prone to control.

Your Leadership relies on:

Your willingness to be **R**esponsible
Your ability to master your **A**ttitude
The strength of your **D**iscipline

Yes, leadership is RAD. The key is to develop yourself by engaging in life, by taking initiative and making things happen. Become the man who steps up and volunteers to get something done when others are silent and paralyzed by their doubt. You are the leader of your life and you will become the leader of your family, so develop yourself by being on the field of life, knowing that today's practice will prepare you for tomorrow's big game.

Confidentiality

A man must be able to keep things confidential, intended to be kept secret. Men's organizations are often criticized for having "secret handshakes." While these rituals may seem foolish to most women, they are very symbolic. If a man can't keep the insignificant things confidential, then how can he be entrusted with significant and private matters? A man's ability to keep something in confidence does reflect on his character. Besides, she doesn't really want to know anyway. She just wants to test her power over you and get you to tell her. If you fail and break this confidence, it will weaken her ability to trust you. Keeping things confidential is an essential discipline for a man.

Pay attention to why you feel compelled to tell your wife or girlfriend everything. If you are honest with yourself, you do it to gain her approval and acceptance. You want her to like you. But telling her only invites her to question what you are doing and why. She doesn't need to know every detail and often she doesn't want to know. Furthermore, *if you tell her everything to get her approval, you deny her the opportunity to trust you.*

Some things need to stay amongst the men. Regrettably, I recognize that more women will read this book than men, so there are other principles that need to be taught that have been omitted from this text. If desired, you can help create a forum for these advanced lessons to be taught, so you can develop the necessary wisdom and understanding to apply them.

Fatherhood

As I mentioned in Chapter One, Fatherhood, becoming a father, is a critically important *'rite of passage'* in a man's life. It is a one-way door and you can't imagine what is on the other side. You must have the courage to experience it for yourself. The only men who say they don't want children are the ones who don't have them. *This is often motivated by a man's doubt and insecurity or his reluctance to have a child dependent on him.* Other men view children as a burden, rather than a blessing. They don't know what they are missing. Are they a lot of work? Yes. Are they worth it? Definitely!

More than marriage, *children help keep a man's selfish desires in check.* It will help you to keep your life on track by focusing on providing for the needs of your children rather than serving your own desires. It is your obligation to your family that, if you allow it, will cause you to become a better man.

Fatherhood is a life-changing character-defining endeavor.

It's About Being the Right Man!

While finding a woman who is compatible with you goes a long way to building a strong foundation for your marriage, it does not guarantee success. There is no perfect woman and I assure you, none of you is perfect either. Marriage isn't about finding the right woman; ***it's about being the right man!*** As discussed earlier, finding a woman who shares your values goes a long way to compensate for your own shortcomings and she will help you overcome your limitations.

Remember, the first step of being the right man is being clear about who you are, what you value and where you are going. If you are clear, then you will attract a woman who wants to go where you are going, a woman who believes in you, a woman who will encourage and inspire you to be your best, a woman who will make sacrifices for you.

Go back to page 16 to the list of Character Traits and make a list for yourself of the qualities that you aspire to develop. Hang it where you can see it every day as a reminder of that man.

Being the right man means allowing your role as a husband and father to shape your character. Marriage has many benefits provided you are willing to do what is required of you. *This means not making decisions based on what you want or don't want, or, worse, on how you feel.* It means challenging yourself to hold yourself to the highest possible standard of conduct regardless of what ANYONE else does or doesn't do. Know what is required of you, and do it, despite your feelings about it.

Don't be too soft on yourself, thinking that you are better than you really are. Again:

The performance of your skills must exceed the opinion of your skills.

Tempered by Life

Why do we temper steel? To make it stronger. How do we temper steel? By sticking it into a raging fire and beating into shape. Just like steel, a man must be tempered in order to shape and mold his character. Instead of fire, we have life. It is the challenges, struggles, and sometimes trauma that a man overcomes in his life that make him strong, that pull forth his best qualities and that shape his character. The Apostle Paul writes in his Letters to the Corinthians, "boast in our suffering, knowing that suffering produces endurance, endurance produces character, and character produces hope... ."[6] Do not run from adversity, understand what it requires of you and bravely step forward.

Regrettably, when faced with a challenge, all too many men have a bad habit of asking themselves what I would refer to as "stupid questions." They are stupid because they only lead a man to hesitate, to doubt, to step back, and to quit. Questions like: "Why me?" or "What if I did or didn't do ...?" Such questions are rooted in looking at life's challenges as a burden. Such questions don't pull a man forward. Instead, they open a back door that allows him to shed accountability for the situation.

What else could you do? What can you ask yourself when faced by challenging circumstances? I have found the most effective questions include, "What does this situation ask of me?" and, "How is this situation preparing me for what's next?" Your character is revealed and only counts when life is difficult. How you respond in the midst of tragedy reveals who you really are as a man!

Life is a powerful teacher and trauma is its most effective instrument. Robert Bly writes in *Iron John*, "A man will give his greatest gift to the world through transcending his deepest pain." This has been true for many as it is for me, and may also be for you. A man I know who grew up in a very bad part of the city wound up spending 10 years as a young adult in prison. Now he invests his time in similar young men, counseling them so they don't make the same mistake.

How a man wrestles with and responds to the tragedy in his life determines if that thing will paralyze him or propel him forward.

If a man can rise above his pain and grief, the tragedy will yield an epiphany about what he values and what he must give his life to.

[6] New King James Bible: Romans Chapter 5 Verse 3

In most cases, it leads men on a path to protect others from experiencing this same trauma. It can be as simple as committing to be a better husband and father than his own was or it can grow into a life's purpose to help others. You don't need to look very far to find dozens of examples and the powerful good that has grown from great loss. How often have you witnessed grieving parents who lost a child to a tragic death find solace in creating charitable organizations designed to protect other families from the same tragedy? What lessons has your life taught you and what will you do with these lessons?

Write Your Own Obituary

When my oldest son turned 18, I gathered some men who are close to us and held a dinner for him. The evening was inspired by Robert Lewis's book *Raising a Modern Day Knight*. Throughout his book, Lewis comments on the importance of ceremony in a man's life. To mark this occasion of my son becoming a man, I had a picture framed and under it is written these words:

When you were born, you cried and the world rejoiced.
Live your life, so that when you die,
the world cries and you rejoice!

What a profoundly powerful message. This charge will lead him forward long after I am gone. What will people say when your time is done?

As a tool to help you set the direction of your life and to keep you on the straight and narrow path, regardless of your age or current circumstances, I charge you to write your own obituary, in two forms.

First write it as you would like it to read at the end of your days. What would you really aspire for others to say about you and the life that you have led? What is the legacy that you will leave? What impact will you have had on the lives of others? What was the purpose and central meaning of your life? Whom did you serve? Once written, this document can be a powerful guide for your future.

Next write your obituary as it would read right now! But don't sugar-coat it, be as honest and as brutally objective as you possibly can. There is no benefit in being soft on yourself, so grade yourself hard. If you are like most men there will be a gap between the two versions of your obituary. For some of you the gap will be greater than for others. Equipped with the understanding of this gap and aware of any regrets you may now have, you can set your sights on closing the gap, on developing your character by adjusting your attitude and your behavior so that you become the man of the first obituary. It's time to get started because none of us really knows how much time we actually have. The silent danger is thinking you have time and procrastinating. Remember, tomorrow never comes!

Why Get Married?

Before you propose to a woman, it is critically important to know why you want to get married and why you are choosing to marry this particular woman. While it is most important to focus on being the right man, the right woman, one who shares your same values, beliefs, and faith, can be an important and powerful ally in your life. While choosing to date a woman because she is hot or good in bed has its short-term benefits, *it is not a viable strategy for a life-long successful marriage.* These are selfish reasons and the benefits will erode over time. Then what? If you plan to have a family, other factors become more important. What kind of mother will she be? Is she loving and nurturing? Can she put others' needs before her own? What does she value most? Does she respect men? How does she manage her money? What is the quality of her parents' relationship and is she confident in herself? A woman who believes in what you believe in will support, encourage, and inspire you, and feed your ego. A good wife is a powerful ally. Her feminine perspective will complement yours and bring strengths where you may have weaknesses.

Conversely, if she doesn't share your beliefs and values, there will be a constant friction in your marriage. Conflicts will emerge with increasing regularity, particularly if you stop getting what you want from her. But you shouldn't get married because you think she's going to do something for you or take care of you. She is not your mother. You should get married because you have compatible values and you both want to create a life together and have a family.

In reality, as my wife joked one afternoon, "Yes, the girls do the choosing, and the boys do the losing!" Just because she chooses you, that does not mean that you should choose her. Remember, her job is to get the best man that she can. *If the women whom you would like to be with are passing you over, pay attention!* As you focus yourself on developing your character and "being the right man" you will attract many women who will choose you.

There are many emotional, physical, and psychological benefits of being married. In 2010, a major survey by Harvard of 127,545 American adults found that married men are healthier than men who were never married or whose marriages ended in divorce or widowhood. As discussed earlier, a man's commitment to protect and provide for his wife and children provides him purpose and requires that he does his best.

Being married requires a man to develop his character, to be committed, disciplined, and self-reliant, to become a man that his wife and children can count on, no matter what. Not surprisingly, these are some of the very same qualities that a man needs in order to be successful in his professional life. You become a man that others can count on, no matter what! Yes, with the proper training and guidance, marriage can cause you to become a better man. It comes with a price, but then again, nothing ventured, nothing gained. The rewards of a successful marriage are priceless.

Your Relationships with Women

What is the quality of your relationships with women? For many men this can be a challenging question but an important one to consider. Your relationship with women begins with most influential woman in your early life, your mother. Your experience with your mother forms the foundation of what you think about women. What was your relationship with your mother as a child? Did you experience your mother's unconditional love or was her love elusive? What is the quality of your relationship with your mother now? Regardless of your beginning, you must be responsible for how you view and treat women.

Is it your nature to care for women or do you expect them to take care of you? Do you only pursue women to get something you want? Is your own identity linked to the woman that you are with? Do you respect women? Are you prepared to care for and protect the women in your life?

How Do You Know That You Are Ready?

One of the defining differences between a boy and a man is:

A boy serves his own needs,
while a man serves something outside of himself.

Given this distinction, where are you on this spectrum? *You are not ready to be married if your life is still about what you want for yourself, and about what you can take from the women and the world around you.* You must have crossed over that threshold where purpose and meaning have replaced happiness and personal pleasure. Remember, purpose leads to fulfillment and pleasure leads to addiction. It always has been and will always be and no man is ever free from this truth. This is not to say that you should not enjoy life; you should. However, it is critically important that you know what the motivating force is in your life.

If you are ready and willing to make the necessary sacrifices for your family and accept that you are no longer number one, if you are clear about the direction of your life, if you have mastered your ego, if you have satiated your desire to pleasure yourself, then you just might be ready. In reality, aside from these few qualifications *you can never really know for certain if you are ready, and if you waited until you thought you were ready, you would never get married.* Until you get married, you have no personal experience of what it is like to be married and the profound impact it has on you. *Living together doesn't count.* You must be willing to do the necessary work to cultivate your character. You must be willing to allow the obligations and responsibilities of being a husband and a father to shape and mold you into a better man. Marriage, as with life itself, is fraught with risk and rewards. This guide will be essential as you navigate these new waters.

Not surprisingly, it again comes back to a matter of attitude. Do you view marriage as burden to be endured for which you are the victim, or do you view marriage as an essential journey of your life in which you become the hero to your family and your community? As Master Chief Randal tells his cadets in the movie, *The Guardian*, the only difference between the hero and the victim is the attitude when you hit the water. Will your attitude lead you to succeed?

Key Thoughts

- The measure of a man is his willingness to be responsible for that which he is not responsible for.
- Your marriage must be built on a foundation of shared values.
- It is not about finding the right woman; it is about *being* the right man!
- A man can't find his identity in a woman, but it can be enhanced by one!
- Love is giving without expectations.
- Love, the noun (feelings), flows from love, the verb (actions).
- If you are being controlled, then you are out of control.

Recommended Actions

- Stay true to your values and attract a woman who shares them.
- Strive to be honorable . . . always, and in all ways!
- Be prepared, by preparing yourself.
- Earn the respect of other men.

Questions for Reflection

1. What is your relationship with money? On what and on whom do you spend your money? Are you willing to provide 100% of your family's financial needs?

2. What kind of man do you seek to be? Make a list of the qualities of character you aspire to have and must develop within yourself.

3. How would your obituary read if you were to die today? What do you intend for it to say at the end of your life?

Chapter Three – Just Married!

Marriage is not about finding the right woman;
it is about being the right man!

What's Different

Prior to the wedding day, both you and your bride are still on your best behavior as you are still trying to win her over and she is doing the same even while the consequences of leaving are relatively small. Unfortunately, once married, you both relax and your behavior can deteriorate back to your actual "normal" behavior. Once married you no longer adopt the attitude needed to win each other; your default attitude begins to seep through. Furthermore, since you now have the girl, over time and without mindful intention, you are prone to stop doing all the things that you did to get the girl in the first place. But don't fret; this is where the real opportunity lies.

It is also important to note that it takes seven to fourteen years for the marriage to take root. It takes time for you and your wife to give up your individual and separate identities and evolve to embrace your spouse and being married as part of your new identity. Your old identity as a single man will not serve your marriage. The sooner you give it up the better it is.

Dependence, Independence and Interdependence

You should never get married if you need something from your wife, if you are dependent on her for anything, especially her approval and acceptance, or for her to take care of you in some way. You must have reached the point in your life where you are independent, self-sufficient, and able to provide for yourself and others. You must be ***disciplined and emotionally stable***. You must have ***your financial house in order*** and be clear about your aspirations in life. But it doesn't stop there. Marriage requires you to take the next step in your development. It requires that you learn how to be and to become interdependent, inseparably connected. Think about that for a moment. That's why just about every culture has something similar to: "What God has joined, let no man put asunder!" Especially not you. Marriage is not an experiment, something to try on and see if it works. It is a powerful life-changing commitment that molds you into the man that you will become.

As you would expect, this is not something that you can do by yourself and it doesn't come naturally. You must work at it. Becoming interdependent in marriage requires that you put your trust in your wife so that you co-operate with her in your life together. Your objective and focus must be on the greater good of your wife, your marriage, and your family - not yourself. What does it take to become interdependent? As with all good commitments, it will require that you make sacrifices. You must subordinate the things you value for yourself, for the sake of something having a more pressing claim.

So perhaps you got married before you read this and no one told you about the importance of interdependence. Now what? Well, the first order of business is to wean yourself from being needy and dependent. No woman wants a needy man. Next, develop discipline in all aspects of your life. Bear in mind it is nearly impossible to do this on your own.

Your Best Behavior

For more on this period of your relationship, read *The First Five Years: Make the Love Investment That Lasts a Lifetime* by Bill and Pam Farrell. They advocate:

"Tough on Me, Tender on You."

This mindset can spare you from many unwarranted and costly conflicts.

Isn't it odd that men and women put their best face (and foot) forward while they are courting? You do all kinds of things for her, you act and/or dress a certain way to gain her favor, and the natural consequence is an abundant feeling of love. You do this for her, and she does this for you. You wine her and dine her. Nothing could be better! Then you get married, you settle in and get comfortable with each other and then WHAM, your REAL identities and personalities begin to emerge. You may begin to notice that it is not as rosy as before. Yes, it is very important to relax and to be comfortable with each other, to enjoy the freedom to be yourself with each other. In fact, it is critically important that you do it before you get married so she can see the real you. However, once married you must continue to deepen the level of care for your wife independent of what she does or doesn't do in return.

If you are single, next time you are courting a woman, just be yourself and see what happens. Courting is not about tricking her into believing you are something you're not. It is about letting her decide if you are the best man for her. You must be certain that she accepts you as is and believes in the man that you aspire to be. If you find yourself saying she wouldn't want to be with me as I am, then work on developing that part of your character, not just the façade.

Instead of being less of a mate than you were while you are courting, you must bring your wife your best; your very best! How wonderful it would be if she were more in love with you after you got married than before, instead of it being the other way around. Shouldn't you get better with age? Doesn't your wife, the one you have chosen, deserve more of you than anyone else? Surprise her and surprise yourself: bring her your best!

If you got married before you found this book, go back and re-read Chapters One and Two to see if you are properly prepared for the responsibilities and obligations that you now have and to identify what gaps you need to close quickly. Are you needy, selfish, prone to anger, undisciplined, or timid? Make a list of the parts of your character that you need to refine and develop a plan to do so.

The Real Commitment Begins

You may have thought you were committed to each other before the wedding, but the formal act of marriage makes the commitment real. You can no longer just go your separate ways; separation becomes much more difficult and ever more painful. Marriage is a true rite of passage that only married men, by their experience, understand. Many men in extended, perhaps exclusive, seemingly committed relationships think that they are committed. In reality, they may be monogamous, but they certainly are not fully committed. The Oxford Dictionary of English defines commitment as: "The state or quality of being dedicated to a cause or activity, an engagement or obligation that restricts freedom of action." You must be dedicated to your marriage and allow that obligation to keep you on the right path, doing the right thing, at the right time. Commitment requires a man to develop self-discipline and willpower. A husband's commitment in marriage provides the wife security in the relationship.

Marriage Won't Make You Happy

If you got married because you think it is supposed make you happy, think again. You and you alone are solely responsible for your happiness. Happiness is a feeling or mindset that you alone control and depending on the attitude you hold the same activity that you think made you happy one day may not the next. No one but you can decide if you are happy and it can never be contingent on what someone else does or doesn't do. **Marriage is NOT about you!** If you still think that life is about you, then you are not mature enough to be married.

With that said, marriage can and should be enjoyable and very rewarding. If you choose wisely and marry a woman with the same values, faith, and path in life, then it will be more enjoyable and more fulfilling than if you marry a woman for other more superficial reasons.

Marriage requires something of you. It requires that you think about the wellbeing of your wife and your future children. It requires that you make sacrifices. It requires you to develop humility, compassion, and responsibility. It requires that you do all kinds of things that you may not want to in the moment, but that are necessary for you to be the husband who will garner your wife's everlasting love and affection. In the long run marriage will make you a better man, but you must be willing to allow your marriage to cultivate your character. If you do, it will be amazing. If you don't, you will be miserable and convince yourself that you have every right to be miserable. So choose wisely.

It is not a Partnership, It's a Union

Contrary to popular thinking, a marriage is not a partnership. Did you know that in business a partnership has the highest risk of failure? This is true in part because the members of the partnership still act like individuals protecting their own personal interests. Each partner is concerned about getting their fair-share and keeping score of what they are investing and what they are receiving in return from that investment. Marriage is not a partnership. A marriage is a union, a joining of two into one, uniting a man and a woman who are all in, 100%. Each must be focused on what is best for their marriage, for their spouse, and ultimately for their children. The sooner you can rid yourself of any residual selfish attitude of 'this is mine', replacing it with 'this is ours', or better yet, 'this is for you', the stronger your marriage will be. For many men, the first real test is with their money. It is also the #1 thing couples fight over, the source of most conflicts. Go back and reread Money Matters in Chapter Two.

Are you willing to give up your separate individual accounts in exchange for one joint household account? If not, you need to look at the real truth of the matter, not your amusing justification. Is your money still ***your*** money? Where else do you hold yourself separate, keep score, or think you are better in some way? Are you still concerned about buying toys or protecting yourself from her? Do you trust your wife with all the money? Can she trust you?

Keeping score financially, 'I paid this, you pay that,' only leads to keeping score elsewhere. Keeping score indicates that you are more concerned about investing more than your fair share or about not being the loser! When you are generous, there is no scoreboard and you can't be taken advantage of.

A man finds value in his ability to win today's game, not from reminiscing about yesterday's victory. A major part of your role is to work hard, master your craft, make the money and do it again. So give it to her and go make some more. It is one of the most honorable ways for a man to provide for and protect his family.

Joint Finances

If you intend to become a union, then you must consolidate your finances. Yes, a single joint checking account - not one for her money, one for my money, and one for household expenses that each of you pays their fair share. If you make more money or bring more assets to the marriage good for you, well done, but it doesn't matter once you are married.

What is yours is now hers and what is hers is now yours.

If you have any concerns about your share of the money, then that is a BIG red flag about the real health of your relationship. To have one future, you need one pocket book. As you build your family there will be no shortage of expenses for apartments, furnishings, cars, homes, vacations, and perhaps children someday. Again, pay attention and ask yourself: "What do I communicate if I hold my money separate?" and "What do I communicate by putting all my chips on the table and being all in?"

I recently spoke with a man from Alabama who is now in his eighties and happily married more than fifty-seven years. While he was still courting his wife, he put her name on his bank account. When he told his then fiancée that he had done that, she remarked, "Why would you do that?" To which he simply replied: "If I cannot trust you with our money *before* we get married, I can't trust you with it *after* we get married."

I have counseled many married men who at first were VERY unwilling to take this step, but each having done so is grateful that he has. If you object to this guidance, you should make a list of your reasons and then read them out loud to yourself. Then ask yourself, would I marry a man who believed this? Then ask yourself, what does this reveal about my commitment to my wife? Failing to combine finances allows you to temporarily avoid dealing with important issues, which at best will impair the intimacy with your wife and at worst be a fatal crack that could destroy your marriage. Neither is worth risking.

Communication

Communication in your marriage is critical and a man is ALWAYS communicating, not with his words, but with his actions. You may foolishly believe that what you say is what you are communicating. It might be what you hope you are communicating or wish that she is hearing, but your actions reveal the truth. Women have a sixth sense of this. They carefully observe your actions and test to see if what you say is 100% aligned with what you do. If your actions are aligned with your words, then your woman can trust you. If they are not, women are astute enough to know that you are lying to them or at least bending the truth. So pay attention! Pay close attention to what your actions are saying about what, and who, is important to you.

That said, you should also have things to talk about with your wife and be sure to listen. For women, communication is the vehicle of relationship. It's how they create a relationship, how they establish their connection with you. Again, their brains are wired differently. So, while this may not be your strong suit, be sure that you have things to talk about. I will expand on this topic later in the book.

Listen with Your Undivided Attention

The most important action a man can take when communicating with a woman is to listen. And since a man can only really do one thing at a time, this means doing nothing other than listening. Yes, turn the TV off, put down your phone, don't be thinking about what you will do when this is over. Don't listen to respond or to solve the problem. Stephen Covey, author of the *The 7 Habits of Effective People* captures this eloquently in Habit #5: Seek first to understand, then to be understood. When your wife feels understood, she feels valued and cared for.

Try it. At first, this will be incredibly difficult because our brains are naturally wired to find the point, fix it, and solve problems. There is a very insightful and humorous video on YouTube that illustrates this point that all men should watch, entitled *It's Not About the Nail* https://www.youtube.com/watch?v=-4EDhdAHrOg. Watch it and this principle will certainly come into focus.

Since women use language to establish their connection, to deepen their relationship with you, here is an important clue:

"The longer she is talking, the less you are listening!"

Ouch! When your wife feels that she is connected, that she has your undivided attention, the talking will subside. But you have to listen with no other agenda or motivation than to listen and to be present with her. For many men this will be a radical change of behavior, so much so that it may initially scare your wife. She may wonder, *"Who are you and what have you done with my husband?"* You will need to reassure her that you just want to listen.

The Five Love Languages - Be Generous

The key to a healthy marriage is not loving your wife in the same way you want to be loved, but to take care of her in the manner that she feels taken care of. Gary Chapman, author of *The 5 Love Languages: The Secret to Love that Lasts,* presents five simple categories of things that you can do to make your wife feel cared for and appreciated. While all are good, every woman has her own preference, as do you, valuing one form slightly more than the others. Understanding these differences will help you do a better job. And if you are like most men, deep down you really want to do a good job. The five love languages are:

Affirmation: Say nice things, be generous with your words and compliments. This requires that you pay attention to your wife. Compliment her in front of her friends. Make her feel important to you. A compliment about who she is and what you appreciate about her is very impactful. When you acknowledge your wife by saying how much you appreciate her love, care, thoughtfulness, insights, etc., you build her self-confidence and self-esteem.

Time: Make time for her, take her places that *she* wants to go. Time is the most precious and limited resource you have. Surprisingly, spending time is quite often the more effective love language. Spending time with her communicates that she is important to you. How nice! Remember, the poor woman just WANTS to be with you. Do not reject her desire to be with you.

Receiving Gifts: Buy her things, things that demonstrate that you know her, her likes, and her desires. While men always enjoy getting tools, buying her household appliances doesn't count: no vacuums, no mixers, no washing machines, etc. Only if she really likes to cook can you buy her a stove, but it better be over-the-top good. Gifts don't always need to be big or extravagant. In fact, it is the thought that counts. Your wife can feel appreciated by the little things just as much with the big things, if they reflect your understanding of what she likes. Stopping on the way home to buy her flowers or her favorite dessert goes a long way to communicating that she is important to you.

Acts of Service: This should be the easiest for a man, because we like to do things. This is taking care of her, her home, her car, her finances. If anything breaks, you fix it. Put gas in her car, take the trash out. Acts of service are best done anonymously. Don't tell her that you are going to do it before you do it. Just do it and keep quiet about it. She will notice on her own. Too many men get themselves into trouble by saying that they are going to do something, all too often motivated to win her approval and acceptance, and then they don't do it! You can spare yourself from this by keeping your mouth shut and just, in the words of Patriots Coach Bill Belichick, "Do your job" with "No Days Off." This wins championships.

Physical Touch: Touch her, but not just when you want to go to bed. Hold her hand, rub her back, be close to her in public. Arouse her desire for you by touching her without expectations of getting anything in return. Engage in physical touch, absent any sexual intentions.

To meet her needs, you must first understand what her primary love language is. To understand what her language is, pay close attention to how she expresses love to you and to others. Also, be alert to what she complains about. Her complaints are actually requests in disguise. They will provide you a clue of what her love language is. Learn her love language and be generous. Remember that you will have a natural tendency to express love in the manner that you wish to receive love. Doing so could be motivated by the right intention, but it may still miss the mark. It takes effort to do things that you know she will appreciate. Remember, you can't win at baseball throwing touchdowns. The right action in the wrong place is still the wrong action.

A man expresses his love for his wife by taking care of her.

Find out how to take care of your wife and then do a really good job at it, better yet be the very best at it. You also need to understand that women are most appreciative when your expressions of love are new and unexpected. Mark Gruber, in his routine on *"How to Reward a Man,"* humorously reveals the importance women place on the unexpected gifts, so challenge yourself to be creative. If you do, other men's wives will complain that their husbands are not nearly as good as your wife's husband. It is better to be that man than not.

You must also be aware of what you do that is the opposite of these. In the same manner that engaging a love language communicates that she is important to you, a void in one or more dimensions has the opposite impact. It communicates that she is not important or that you have taken her for granted in some way. So do not neglect any area in the process or you will leave her feeling neglected. Which area might you be neglecting? When is the last time you did something out of the ordinary or exceptionally generous for her, for no reason, just because?

Know what your own preference is as well and TELL her. How would she know if you don't let her know? After all, the lovely lady is just trying to have a relationship with you. Don't make it any more difficult than it already is. Furthermore, she too needs to have the experience of being loving. So help her out, find things that she can do for you that will percolate her feeling of love towards you. The caveat is that you can't get your feelings hurt or be resentful if she doesn't do them, and you must be appreciative if she does.

Lastly, it is a bonus if you are fortunate enough to have similar preferences. Just don't forget about the other four love languages.

Co-Operate with Your Wife

Co-operate, don't compromise yourself! Despite what she says to the contrary, every woman needs a man that she can't control. As mentioned in Chapter Two, this is critically important for her security in the relationship. Unfortunately, the only way that she can know for sure if she can control you is to try. It is her job to try and it is your job not to be controlled. This can be a challenge once you are married. It didn't matter so much before you were married because the relationship was not permanent. Once married, you may be more keenly aware of her tendencies to see if she can control you and if you are ill prepared it will be a source of unnecessary struggle and conflict.

That doesn't mean that if she asks you to take out the trash, you don't do it. Remember, this could be an act of service if you recognized that it needed to be taken out before she asked you. If you are in the middle of something and can't respond to her request in the moment, then let her know when you will take care of it, if you will, and then be certain that you do take care of it.

I charge you to co-operate. The Oxford dictionary defines it as "work jointly towards the same end." Just as it sounds: co and operate. You must always operate together to build, contribute to, and strengthen your marriage. This attitude creates synergy, creating a union that is discernably greater than the sum of the parts. Our differences complement each other, provide perspective, cover our respective blind spots, compensate for our weaknesses and make us better together. This is the principle of synergy when the union is greater than the sum of the parts.

The verb "compromise" on the other hand is defined as to "settle a dispute by mutual concessions." First of all, if you are actively and intentionally working jointly to the same end, then there is little room for disputes. But when one or both of you is putting your own needs above the needs of the relationship, then conflict is certain to occur. When that happens, compromise requires concessions by one or both parties. With concessions, again the dictionary guides our understanding: "a thing that is granted, especially in response to demands." One or both of you winds up worse off, not better off. You may feel cheated and the seed of resentment may begin to grow in the marriage. Make no mistake, you have no right to make demands on your wife.

Sacrifice is defined as to "give up something valued for the sake of something else regarded as more worthy." When you are consciously working toward the same end, then the needs of the marriage, the family, the children, are more worthy than any personal wants or selfish desires. Motivated by the attitude of cooperation, it is easy to offer the gift of sacrifice. And your character is revealed through what and for whom you will make sacrifices. What do your actions reveal about your character?

Always take care of your responsibilities and help her with what you can. Notice what she is doing and offer your hand. Do this, not because you expect some reward, but because it is the honorable thing to do and satisfies one of the Love Languages.

The Link Between Self-Discipline and Intimacy

Your wife's security is rooted in the depth of your self-discipline.

I can't stress this point enough. The greater your self-discipline, the greater the security that you provide, the greater the intimacy you will receive from your wife! Intimacy is the very best fruit of being married. There are several definitions and uses of the word discipline which can lead to negative connotations or feelings about the word. Yes, discipline can mean applying a consequence for inappropriate behavior, but it also is a tool for "Instructing or teaching intended to mold the mind and character and instill a sense of proper, orderly conduct and action; training to behave or act in a controlled and effective manner; mental, intellectual, moral, or spiritual training or exercise." You can create disciplines or practices to develop your character, to keep your attitude in shape and focused on the proper objective.

In layman's terms, self-discipline is determined by your ability to:

Do what is required of you,
when it is required of you,
despite how you happen to feel about it.

Self-discipline is the essence of you being in control of yourself, of mastering your will so that you give your best. If you are disciplined, controlled by your responsibilities and obligations, then you will provide your wife and your future children security. If you are controlled by lesser things, then she is at risk. There are countless examples of undisciplined men who become successful, who become seduced by their success and then they squander it all away.

Discipline is the single most important attribute of a man's character. If you searched Amazon books on the topic self-discipline, you would find over 74,000 results, over 8,000 of which are directed towards success in business. How much time have you invested in developing your own self-discipline? How often do you blow up or lose control of yourself and your emotions? On a scale of 1 to 10, how would you rate your level of self-discipline relative to where you need it to be in order to become the best husband and father you can be? What do you need to do to close that gap?

What do you or can you do to strengthen this muscle? It need not be anything complicated, just something that you will do regularly. More than fifteen years ago, I decided that I would do one more push-up than my age every weekday, before I get into the shower. Now just because Nancy needs me to be disciplined doesn't mean that she comes out and says it. Quite the opposite, she subconsciously and sometimes, not too subtly, tests my discipline. She will "help" me by tickling me, or standing over me, or other similar things. She often says, "This is stupid. How long are you going to do this?" Now the uninformed man might use logic to explain the logic of his actions, or he might become defensive, or worse, in an effort to gain her acceptance, stop all together. My response is and always will be playful: "Just stick with me babe, because when I'm 100, I'll be buff." I had to learn to appreciate her efforts to dissuade my discipline as a way to help me to become more disciplined and steadfast in my resolve.

Nearly anything can become a discipline. Any specific activity that you do for a specific frequency, time, and duration may qualify. It is important to be specific so it is clear that you did or didn't do it. Pay attention to when you do and don't follow through on your discipline. Oh, and don't be surprised when your wife points out when you miss.

Be Playful

Have fun, enjoy, even dare to celebrate your time with your wife. Being playful, not to be confused with being irresponsible, is an essential quality that a man brings to a relationship. Being playful reminds your wife that you are self-confident, secure, and everything is and will be ok. This is very attractive to a woman. Faced with the challenges of life, a man's ability to be playful demonstrates his trust in himself and his abilities. Take what you do seriously; just don't take yourself too seriously.

For a man, life is a game of "Things happen and I'll take care of it" and I will have fun in the process. Being playful is an attitude or a mindset that shapes the context of your life. You can do it, bring it on!

Answer the Question Again, Again, and Again!

When your wife asks you, "Do you love me?" don't be the man who responds, "I told you when we got married that I love you and I would let you know if anything changes. .... Nothing's changed!"

One of my good friends and early mentor has coached hundreds of men for forty years now. He taught me a long time ago that in every interaction with my wife that I should answer the question: 'Do you love me?' While I have all too often failed to execute on his directive, when I do, it is always good. I am reminded about the classic love story that plays out between Tevye and Golde in the timeless tale of *The Fiddler on the Roof*. If you haven't seen it, take your lovely bride to it or rent it some Friday evening. Deep into the storyline, after many of the girls have married and moved away, Tevye asks his wife, "Do you love me?" As Golde recounts all the things she has done for Tevye for so many years, she stops and reassures Tevye that she does. Be certain to answer that question for your wife with steadfast determination. Yes, that means each and every day, with a welcoming embrace, a passionate kiss, or unexpected gift.

Here's a clue: use what you just learned about the Five Love Languages to answer the question 'Do you love me?' in the way your wife understands. Take care of her in some way, make sure everything in the home is working and fix anything that breaks, buy her the occasional gift or flowers, spend time with her, compliment her, and hold her hand when you kiss her before you go. A good dose of each and a double of the one that she values the most. These simple actions go a LONG way!

Treat her like a lady!

I am often reminded by the memorable words from Tom Jones' hit, *She's a Lady*: "Always treat her with respect..."-to do just that. Many men do a great job courting their women while they are dating. They take them out, buy them gifts, spend time with them, hold the door for them; everything is new and unexpected. But once they get married and real life kicks in, they stop, leaving the poor woman left wondering "What's happened? Where did the man who courted me go?" Worse, some men start treating their wives like a man, and not surprisingly they don't like it when their wife starts acting like one. "Treat *your* wife the way *your* wife deserves to be treated." Be a gentleman, be generous and don't neglect her.

Your job is to take care of her, and how well you do reveals a great deal about your character. What do your actions reveal about the man that you have become?

Date Your Wife

Gary Rosberg, author of *40 Unforgettable Dates with Your Mate,* challenges men to continue the behavior they exhibited when they won their wife in the first place. Remember, she just wants to be with you, so make it worth her while. Continue to pursue her and think creatively. It need not be complicated or expensive, just make time to be together. Although it may not be in our nature to be creative, it can be fun. If needed, designate a specific night and protect it. If you have young children, get a babysitter and leave the kids home.

The Safety Tip

Okay gentlemen, so far so good. This next point may be very hard for some of you to accept; but you must!

"Whenever you experience your wife as anything less than completely loving, it is her gift to you reminding you that you are not being the man you can be!"

Ouch! No, I'd rather criticize her for being difficult, and then use her bad behavior as an excuse for my own. Anyone tried that? How did it go? I expect not very well.

I have spent nearly two decades coaching other men, and more than a decade ago, I had just offered this "advice" to another man one night, only to find myself needing it the very next morning. We were buying a new home and it was a financial stretch, but we decided to 'go for it'. On my way to work, I spoke with our broker only to find out that another couple had just made, moments before, a full price non-contingent offer on the house we wanted. Our home was not even on the market and the thought of a non-conditional offer was entirely out of the question. So naturally and logically, I folded, conceding the home to the other family. Not thinking too much about it, I called my wife to tell her. To my surprise, she laid into me. I don't recall exactly what she said I just remember holding the phone away from my ear and thinking to myself who is this woman? Fortunately, my own counsel was still wrestling around my head from the night before.

Very importantly, I did not escalate the conflict by attacking her behavior or by using logic to defend myself. Instead, I asked myself, what is it about me that she is reacting to? She had never seen me fold before. When we bought the house we were in, she saw me jump through hoops, leading the mortgage broker through the process to get the deal done. This time, that man was nowhere in sight. This is what Nancy was reacting to. Luckily since I chose not to throw gasoline on the fire, by the time I got home she was extremely apologetic and said something very intriguing "I knew what I was doing, but I couldn't stop." It was an emotional reaction.

What can you do to prepare yourself for a possible negative response? First, pay attention, notice your own bad behaviors, recognize when they are rearing their ugly heads. Second, seek the counsel of other men. Often when you discuss the specific circumstances with another man, you will discover what to do in the process. When in doubt, be generous.

You must accept this essential lesson: "Whenever you experience your wife as anything less than completely loving, it is her gift to you reminding you that you are not being the man you can be!" If you can focus on yourself and vigilantly strive to do and be your best, it will transform your marriage, your family, and your life.

Build Hedges to Protect Your Marriage

The stronger you become as a man, the greater the temptations you will experience. Jerry B. Jenkins presents a power metaphor in his book *Hedges: Loving Your Marriage Enough to Protect It*, 2006. A hedge is a boundary or barrier that keeps things out and protects what is within the walls of the hedge. Jenkins suggests that you build hedges around your marriage to keep temptation out and protect it from harm. A man's role is to protect, so it only seems natural that he protects his marriage. How can you protect your marriage? Just asking the question causes you to think differently about this job that you may have neglected without even knowing it.

First, you can protect it from the outside dangers by avoiding potentially compromising situations. This can be as simple as not dining or traveling alone with another woman. This could also include not disclosing any marital or personal issues to another woman. Ever notice that a man is often in a new relationship with another woman before he divorces his current wife? Most started with small seemingly harmless interactions, but grew with gradual increases in intimacy. When men stray it is nearly always physical, so you can protect your marriage by eliminating the opportunity for temptation. Protecting yourself and your marriage requires discipline and self-control. Don't put yourself into situations where you know you will be unnecessarily tested and tempted.

Second, accountability to another man can be a very powerful hedge. *If you establish true accountability with another married man to whom you agree to disclose all your actions, this alone can keep you on the right path.* You must be willing to tell him everything, *especially the things you don't want to tell him.* Just knowing that you will have to make an account of your actions is enough to alter your behavior towards the honorable actions that you intend.

Third, you must protect it from within. When women stray it is nearly always emotional. You can protect your marriage by being grateful for and generous towards your wife. She must know that she is the only woman that you desire. Tending the hedge requires attention to it each and every day. Make certain to treat her the best of all. I tease men about being more flirtatious with the girl who pours their coffee at the local coffee shop than they are with their wives. It gets a chuckle, but then the truth of it sinks in. If you neglect your wife, you are neglecting your marriage. Continue to deepen your care for and commitment to your wife. Don't take her for granted. *Your wife should always get your very best.*

Key Thoughts

- Marriage, honorably served, forces you to become a better man!
- Every woman needs a man whom she can't control.
- Remember, the poor woman is just trying to have a relationship with you. Don't make it any harder than it already is!
- Did I mention that Love is a verb?

Recommended Actions

- Develop uncompromising self-discipline.
- Know your wife's love language.
- Answer the question: "Do you love me?" in EVERY interaction.
- Keep dating your wife...for the rest of your life!
- Treat *your* wife the way *your* wife deserves to be treated.
- Be grateful and very generous.
- Be playful: Take what you do seriously, not yourself.
- Make her look good by being the best man you can be.

Questions for Reflection

1. Is your money still your money? What else are you holding separate? Where are you keeping score?

2. On a scale of 1-10, how disciplined are you compared to where you need to be?

3. What sacrifices do you willingly make for the marriage? What are you unwilling to sacrifice?

4. To whom will you be accountable for ALL your actions and when will you begin?

5. Develop a list of character traits that you aspire to possess and list the steps you will take to develop them.

Chapter Four – Married with Children

"It's really not about you!"

Everything Changes

When you married, two became one, a couple. You were able to enjoy each other's company without the demands and distractions of children with a lot of time left over for yourself. When first married, the demands on you didn't increase that much because your wife could largely take care of her own needs. At times, time seemed to stand still, each day was largely like the day before, and the day before that.

Once you have children, your wife becomes a mother and you become a father. Your responsibilities expand greatly to raise, nurture, educate, provide for and protect this new child and hopefully more children. It is very natural for your wife to turn her attention and care towards her children. This means that she will have less time and energy to focus on you; get over it! A needy or insecure man may feel neglected and even resentful, but remember they are the children: they need her; you don't. It is a good time for you to become more self-confident and self-sufficient.

The Commitment Just Got Bigger

While you may think that you will be married for a lifetime, children bring an irreversible permanence to your relationship as you transition from a couple to become a family. Becoming a father is another *critical* rite of passage in a man's life. You may recall Michael Phelps, the most decorated Olympian of all time. In an interview during the 2016 Olympics, he described how becoming a father had changed his game. Honorably served, your obligations and responsibilities as a husband and father will further the development of your character. If you allow it, these obligations should cause you to rid yourself of the remaining vestiges of being a needy little boy in a man's clothing. If you don't, your marriage will suffer and your children will pay the price for your selfishness.

Your obligations and responsibilities as a father to a son will cause you to become clear about what it means to be a man and to become a better man yourself. It is critical, so that you can teach your son how to be a good man, not through what you say, but by what you do and do not do! Your role as a father to a daughter will cause you to show her what a good man looks like as exemplified by and through your behavior. They are watching you; they are always watching.

Would you be proud if your son emulated your character and values? Are you confident that your son can make it on his own? Would you be excited if your daughter brought a man home who was ***just*** like you? If you can't honestly and objectively say 'yes', then this is your wakeup call before it is too late.

The Father's Mindset

There are two key beliefs or attitudes that have served me as a father. The first is:

If my children don't think I am the most disciplined man on the planet, then I have work to do.

And the second is equally challenging:

There are no such things as bad children, just bad parents.

The critical element of these principles is that they place all the responsibility squarely on my shoulders. It keeps me single-mindedly focused on my attitude and actions, and it guards me against placing blame elsewhere. Are you willing to accept these two guiding principles? Truly, the only thing we can control is ourselves. Your willingness to accept and serve these responsibilities reveals a great deal about you.

The Critical Importance of the Father

According to the 2017 US Census, 19.7 million children live without a father in the home. That is over 25% of all children. 33% of the children live without their biological father in the home. Children who are raised in a father-absent home suffer:

- 4x greater risk of poverty
- 7x more likely to become a pregnant teen
- More likely to have behavioral problems
- More likely to abuse drugs and alcohol
- 2x more likely to suffer from obesity
- 2x more likely to drop out of high school
- More likely to commit a crime
- More likely to suffer abuse and neglect

These facts are corroborated by the US Justice Department's and US Department of Health and Human Services' findings about fatherless homes:

- 85% of youth inmates grew up in fatherless homes
- 63% of youth suicides are children living in fatherless homes
- Even when poverty levels are equal, children who come from a two-parent home outperform children who come from a one-parent home.

The research is clear: fathers factor significantly in the lives of their children. There is simply no substitute for the love, involvement, and commitment of a responsible father.

While humans are not elephants, the parallel is striking. In 2000, Lucy Freeman from BBC Earth reported that Gus Van Dyk, an ecologist at Pilanesberg National Park, South Africa, was worried by a series of attacks on the park's rhino. More than 50 had been mutilated and killed and the cause was unknown. He soon discovered that the culprits were an "out-of-control gang of elephants, between 15 and 18 who were in musth." These elephants had been transported to the park with their mothers and siblings, but without older male elephants. "As a result, there were no older bull elephants to push these youngsters out of musth. ... The huge rush of testosterone was overwhelming them and driving them to aggressive behaviour."

Gus Van Dyk theorized that the problem was the missing male elephants and he was right. Six large bulls were introduced from Kruger National Park, who towered over the adolescents, and ***literally within hours***, the teen thugs had dropped out of musth. No more rhinos have since been killed by rampaging youngsters."

The emotional, physical, psychological, financial, and spiritual consequences of a fatherless home are unmistakable in the wild and at home. The security, guidance, and leadership of the father can't be replaced.

Engage a Qualified Mentor and Heed his Counsel

My favorite motivational clip is a six-minute segment called The Death Crawl, from a movie titled *Facing the Giants* from Sherwood Pictures. I encourage you to find it on YouTube.com and watch it several times. The death crawl is an exercise for a football lineman to strengthen his arm and leg muscles by putting a running back on his back and then crawling on his arms and legs for 10-20 yards. In this short video an athlete named Brock Kelley has resigned himself to the prospects that his team, the Shiloh Eagles, will lose this coming Friday night's football game to a formidable opponent, Westfield. The coach leads Brock to redefine his best by doing the Death Crawl exercise again, this time blindfolded.

For this to happen, two things are needed. First, Brock must have the courage to allow Coach Grant Taylor to push him past where he quits on his own. He trusts the coach's leadership and follows his instructions. He could have quit at any point and given up because it was too hard. But he doesn't quit. He puts his trust in his coach and allows Coach Taylor to lead him past the point where he would quit on his own.

Second, Coach Taylor embodies five key mentoring qualities:

Companionship, Counsel, Encouragement, Challenge, and a Call to Action

I contend that these five qualities are instrumental in achieving exceptional results from those you lead in your home and everywhere. Companionship: the coach never leaves his side. Counsel: the coach blindfolds Brock so he doesn't quit when he thinks he has given his best. Encouragement: Coach Taylor resounds "you're doing good, keep going." Challenge: when the exercise gets really hard and Brock is preparing his justifications for quitting, the coach pipes out: "It's not too hard…" and "then you negotiate with your body to find more strength" and "don't quit, don't quit." Men need the challenge of other men not to quit. And finally, the call to action is as important as the prior four elements. At the end of the clip, when the coach asks Brock Kelley: "Can I count on you!" Counting on a man calls him forward, literally pulls him past where he quits on his own. A man needs to be counted on by other men, by his wife, and by his children. This is equally true for young men, that they need to be counted on.

Perhaps this should have come earlier in the book. *If you have not done so already, now is the time to seek the counsel and guidance of a mentor,* another man who has successfully navigated the life challenges you now find yourself in. It is natural to have a coach for sports or a mentor at work; why not have one for the most important aspects of your life, your role as a husband and father. He must be a strong man who will listen to you, but not someone who will allow you to place blame elsewhere. It must be someone who will hold you responsible and accountable to a higher standard, someone whom you can and will trust. This man should have acquired objectively observable proficiency as a husband and father. This man must not be concerned about being good to you, just good for you. Not all medicine is easy to swallow, but you must.

Your mentor needs to be objective and help you see the entire situation. When life is hard, he will dust you off, give you a bit of advice, and send you back onto the field of life. When things are good, he will also help you remember how blessed and fortunate you truly are, lest you forget. Lean not on your own understanding, but on someone more experienced and proficient than yourself. To ensure you get the most from your mentor, you **must** do as Brock did. You must have the courage to allow him to push you past where you quit on your own. This means accepting his counsel, especially when you don't want to or when you think it is too hard.

No man knows what his best really is,
he only knows what his last best was.

Your best lies past the point where you quit. We all need someone who cares enough about us, as Coach Taylor cares for Brock Kelly, to push us past where we quit on our own, so that we continually redefine our best!

Your Marriage is the Foundation of the Family

There has been much debate these days about what makes a family. The quality of the relationship that you have with your wife is the foundation, the very bedrock of your family. It is in the love and security of this union where your children find their security and discover an understanding of true love and acceptance.

"Children who develop social and emotional capacities in the first years of life are better prepared to be self-confident, trusting, empathic, inquisitive and communicative as well as capable of relating well to others. In other words, social and emotional health is considered the best foundation for mental, emotional and physical wellness."[7] The most formative source of a child's environment is his or her own family.

Good or bad, but hopefully good: how you care for your wife is how your children will care for others, especially their mother.

The Only Way to Be a Good Father is to Be a GREAT Husband

This is perhaps ***the*** most important lesson to accept as a husband and a father. Unfortunately, if you have failed as a husband, this will be the hardest to accept, but I implore you to move past your emotional reaction and look objectively at this truth. If you take great care of your wife, she will take exceptional care of your children and she will do a much better job than you, so let her do it. Looking back on my own family, I am amazed and humbled by the impact I have been able to have on the quality of the relationship that my children have with their mother. My daughters never had

[7] KidCareCanada.org

the expected contentious teenage years of conflict with their mother and my boys step up and take care of their mother and sisters when I am away.

If you love your children, you must learn to love your wife with deliberate intention and without expectations. If you take great care of your wife, this will set the standards for how your children will take care of and respect their mom. There is no greater gift that you can give to your children or to your wife than for them to have a close and loving relationship. And having learned how to care for others at home, your children will bring this spirit into their own relationships and interactions with other people. *Everybody wins!*

The opposite dynamic is also equally true: if you disrespect and treat your wife poorly, she will treat your children poorly and they in turn will treat her poorly. If you notice that your children are being disrespectful to their mother, it is because you have taught them that that is acceptable or at least permissible, by your actions. If you are self-centered in your attitude in your marriage, you teach your children to be selfish. Everybody loses. I believe the recent increase in "bullying" among children is a direct result of children coming from broken and unloving homes. From homes where the parents act like children, placing their own needs above the needs of the children, while at the same time expecting the children to act like adults. How will you lead your household? What kind of example are you and will you be for your children?

All too often, when tension or conflict arise in a marriage, which will happen, most men, instead of taking responsibility for and resolving the conflict, turn their attention away from their wives and toward their children. Yes, it is possible that your wife may be guilty of this as well, but that's no excuse. This is tragic. The man physically and emotionally turns his attention towards his children, while at the very same time he turns his back on his wife. This act only fuels the conflict and feeds the separation in the marriage because the man communicates, by his actions, that the children are more important. The message is that if it were not for the children, I wouldn't be here with you.

Your Actions Speak Louder Than Your Words

It is always important for you to pay attention to your own actions, your actual observed behaviors, and what they reveal about you and your values. *This is the most honest reflection of your character*, and so much more than what you think, or would like to think, about yourself. If you haven't developed this ability, the wonderful thing about children is they will be excellent assistants in this area. They will exhibit all of your worst and occasionally some of your best behaviors. If you notice that they aren't behaving particularly well, it is a great reminder to look in the mirror and examine how you have taught them to behave.

There no such thing as bad children, just bad parents.

Thinking that your children are the problem, rather than the quality of your marriage or your parenting skills, is a guarantee that you will continue to have more problems. However, if you are willing to take responsibility and adjust your behavior, your home life can quickly change for the better.

The very best compliment that I have ever received from my oldest son was a dozen years ago when we were at Disney World on a family vacation. My son had purchased a few items for his then girlfriend who was back home. Noticing this, my wife trying to be playful was needling him about the fact he was going to "spoil the girl." After about 15 minutes of this, my son had had enough and he snapped back and said firmly, "And where do you think I learned it!" He learned to care for his girlfriend from how I cared for his mother.

A decade later, I now watch how well he cares for his wife and that ensures me that this legacy of caring will continue for generations to come.

If you want to know what you are teaching your children, you only need to look at your actions. It doesn't matter how old they are, your children are always watching you. What are your actions teaching your sons about how to be a man and how to care for a woman? What are you teaching your daughters about men and what they can expect from them? Can she put her trust in a man? Children who disrespect their mothers didn't teach themselves. If it occurs, it is your job to stop it.

Percolate Her Desire for You!

From the first time you laid eyes on your future bride to be, your relationship progressed through twelve stages of intimacy. Some of you may have moved slowly, while others may have moved more swiftly, but all of you progressively increased the intimacy in your marriage. *(More on the twelve stages of intimacy in a moment.)* As the couple becomes a family, it is natural for your wife, now the mother of YOUR children, to turn her focus and attention to the children. Before marriage and certainly before children, you received 100% of your wife's attention.

Now instead of being resentful of this decrease in attention, it is time for you to step up and take the initiative and lead. The metaphor of "percolate" may be lost on many of our younger men who aren't familiar with a percolator. A percolator brews coffee by heating water to a boil and then having it slowly and repeatedly drip water over the basket of fresh coffee grounds. This method takes time and brews a rich flavorful cup of coffee. To fuel her affection towards you, you must constantly be percolating her desires and then patiently waiting. Do something kind for her each day, consistently, regardless of her response. When the time is right for her, she will let you know that she wants to be with you!

Another metaphor for the difference between men and women is that of a crockpot and a wok. A woman is like a crockpot that cooks slowly all day but the meat is tender, moist, and juicy. Pulled pork is best slow-cooked in a crock pot. A man is like a wok: just place it on a fire and it is instantly hot, searing whatever is placed within it. If you turn the crockpot on in the morning with a kiss, an extra-long embrace, a particularly appreciative thank you, then she will think of you throughout the day and be eager to welcome you home. Better still, she will spend her day telling her friends how wonderful you are.

Continue to Pursue Her

I challenged you in Chapter Four to continue to Date Your Wife. Now with the added responsibilities of children and being the provider for your family, it is easy to be caught up with life and to forget to live. When your wife was single, she was pursued by perhaps many men. Now it's only you, you are all she has. Help her remain secure in her relationship with you by continuing to make her feel desired, special, and cared for. You certainly don't want another man to do it, nor do you want her to seek reassurance elsewhere because you have neglected your responsibilities. Make her feel desired by wanting to be with her. Take the lead. Don't ask her, lead.

Twelve Stages of Intimacy

Intimacy between a man and a woman progresses through twelve discernable stages from nothing to the most intimate connection and bonding: sex. With each stage, the depth of vulnerability and trust extended by your wife grows, so treat it with the respect and care that it deserves.

In most men's minds, once they have done the hard work necessary to reach the pinnacle, they think they can go straight back to the pinnacle, skipping all the intermediary stages. This is quite understandable, because that is what he would want her to do; he's a wok. We each have a natural tendency to expect our wife to respond the way that we would respond. I am reminded again of a skit from *Defending the Caveman*, the longest running solo play in Broadway history, where the woman in the story is massaging a man's back trying to be close to him. She asks her man: "How am I doing?" to which the man responds, "good, but you are two feet too high and on the wrong side!" So pay attention to how your wife is with you. If she takes her time, this is a clue for how she wants you to be with her. Remember the old adage, foreplay begins in the kitchen.

Some men complain that they don't get enough sex and continue by saying, "When I touch her, she immediately pulls back." Her reaction is often the by-product of years of training on his part. If the only time you touch your wife is when you want sex, you have conditioned her to relate your touch with you wanting to have sex. So, the very moment you touch her, she hears this as you want to have sex. If she is not prepared or she is not ready at that moment, she will very naturally pull away. If you are an insecure man, you may be prone to feel rejected and you will likewise respond accordingly with behavior that shows you are hurt, frustrated, and/or angry. Instead of a moment that could have brought you closer, your response drives a wedge between you, leaving each of you blaming the other for the breakdown of intimacy in your relationship.

You should consider the eleven stages that precede intercourse as foreplay. They are the basic building blocks for intimacy and they should be practiced and mastered with the same intensity that you have invested in mastering the twelfth stage. These twelve stages are very useful for percolating her desire for you. As you read through them, do so slowly. Pause for a moment after each step and remember when this occurred between you and your wife. Breathe new life into that experience and renewed intimacy into your marriage. Endeavor to practice and master the eleven stages that precede the final stage. The twelve stages were originally published in 1971 by Desmond Morris in his works *Intimate Behavior: A Zoologist's Classic Study of Human Intimacy*. I present a layman's version in the text below:

1: Eye to Body: Intimacy begins within you. Remember the first time you laid eyes on her. The first time she 'caught your eye', remember what it was about her that attracted you to her, that stirred your desire to be with her. Close your eyes for a moment and remember that time. It's good to remember and it is good to steal glances of her without getting caught.

2: Eye to Eye: This is when your eyes connect and she looks back into your eyes engaged and connected. When you look at her now, are your looks still engaging and inviting? Or do your eyes communicate something else? Be mindful of what you say with your eyes. Take the time to look into her eyes.

3: Voice to Voice: Remember the first time you spoke, the sound of her voice, the emotions in her words. When you speak to your wife, be kind, encouraging and complimentary. In the words of Thumper's dad from *Bambi*, "If you can't say anything nice, don't say nothing at all!" Be generous: she will want to talk more than you do since it is her way of having a relationship with you. Pay attention to the attitude conveyed by your tone of voice and listen to her.

4: Hand to Hand: Of the five senses, touch is critically important and often overlooked. Do you hold her hand? When you do, particularly in public, it communicates that you want to be with her, that she is important to you. Hold her hand in the car while driving. Create opportunities to hold her hand and percolate her desire for you.

5: Hand to Shoulder: Intimacy continues to grow as the level of touch increases. As you put your hand on her shoulder you are drawn closer to her and she to you. Let her feel your strength and be comforted by you.

6: Hand to Waist: As you progress, you put your hand on her waist, drawing her ever so close to you. You and she can feel the intimacy grow. Slow down, there's no rush. It's time to go back to step 1 again, before proceeding.

7: Face to Face: Gaze into her eyes, you need not speak, just gaze. Notice the details and beauty of her face. Let your cheek touch hers, your head gently rest upon hers.

8: Hand to Head: Letting someone touch your head is an act of submission. As you touch her, be gentle, caress her cheeks, touch her hair, take the time to know the feel of her skin.

9: Hand to Body: As you progress past the head down to the body, the intimacy continues to grow. Again, take your time, slow down, and allow her anticipation to take over.

10: Mouth to Body: Kiss the girl! Slowly, gently and patiently.

11: Touching below the waist: Third Base. Approach her as if it were the first time.

12: Intercourse: You would be wise to only have sex with your wife *when you have something to give*. Sex in a marriage is just like everything else in your marriage. It is about how well you care for your wife and her needs rather than worrying about your own. Only touch her if you have something to give. If you develop this mindset, then she will be drawn to desire you and certain to reciprocate.

In the words of the band Foreigner, make each time "Feel like the first time!" I assure you, if you play at the low end of the intimacy scale, you will discover that she will begin to pursue you. It is another way to satisfy her love languages of touch and time.

The Game

One day, when the children were still young, I returned home after a long day at work. As usual, the children came running to the door jubilantly exclaiming, "Daddy's home, daddy's home!" Looking down the hall into the family room, I noticed that they had just dropped mom like a hot potato. In a rare moment of inspiration, I turned the children around and brought them back to my wife, kissed her and then the kids. Ever since then, my wife gets the last kiss when I leave and the first kiss when I return home, even if I am just running out for a ten-minute errand. It is funny to watch my youngest daughter go to great lengths to steal the last kiss, but even then I am resolute and my wife gets the last when I leave. Often it means me going back into the house to do so.

I expanded this into what has now come to be known in my home as "The Game". Simply put, Nancy, my wife, my children's mother, is responsible for EVERYTHING that is good in the home, and she gets the credit. If we stop for ice cream, the mantra is "thank your mother." If we go to dinner, go somewhere nice on vacation, get signed up for sports camp, their mantra resounds "Thank you Mom!" Thinking they are smart the children will occasionally add "and Dad." Occasionally my wife will protest saying "your father did it." Nevertheless, while everyone knows it is a game, everyone enjoys The Game just the same.

The unforeseen benefits of The Game are many. First, it elevates mom in the eyes of the children, which makes her feel good, and if mom feels good she will continue to do a great job caring for our children. Another benefit is that it keeps me from being seduced by my ego. It would be easy to think too highly of myself, as the one who provides the financial resources to do all these fun things.

Every man's Achilles Heel is being seduced by the power afforded to him by his position.

My role is not more important than my wife's and this helps keep me in check. Without The Game, my ego could lead me astray.

The fun part is that my adult children have continued The Game. My middle son will make his mom her favorite breakfast and then say "Thank you Mom!" I have taught dozens of other men 'The Game' and they have shared in its benefits and the profound impact on the emotional well-being of their children. Hopefully, it will become a movement.

Don't Blink

Time passes increasingly fast. Ever notice that summer lasted forever when you were five and now it flies by with breakneck speed? While time always ticks away at an eternally predictable rate, statistically speaking, each day is an increasingly less significant portion of the life you've lived. A day when you are five is 1/1,825 of your life; when you are thirty is its 1/10,950; and by the time you are 50 it is 1/18,250. Time may have moved slowly before you had children, but now there is a constant daily reminder of time passing. Make certain you don't waste this time. You only get one shot at it;

there are no do-overs, no mulligans, and no second chances. So live life with a sense of urgency, intention and determination; do your best and be sure you live without regrets!

You Have to be the Bad Guy - Get over it!

In every parental relationship there is critical need for someone to not just set, but to enforce the boundaries and standards of the household. This is your responsibility. Get over it. Boundaries and consequences provide your children with the security they need and teach them valuable life lessons. Mothers often struggle with enforcing the boundaries they set. You can support her by ensuring your children respect her authority as they do yours. Even if she doesn't enforce her own rules, you should. Remember to lead by example.

That said, you must be responsible at all times. I was taught the importance of this lesson by Uncle Paul when my oldest was born. He sat me down and made it vividly clear that as a father I should know two things when giving punishments for bad behavior. First, that the child will do it again, and second, that I must follow through on whatever consequence I provided. If I ever said "If you do that again, I will break your arm!" I knew that I must break my child's arm when they do it again. Now I always thought that my uncle was tough, but as a new parent, I thought as you might be thinking now, that he was a bit extreme.

The REAL lesson is that I had to be responsible for ensuring that the imposed consequence matched the offence. I could not make idle threats that I would not or could not keep; nor could I abdicate my responsibility to shape and mold their character, to teach them that our actions always have consequences. This understanding forced me to be in control and to keep my word. After some discernment, I realized that productive "arduous" labor worked best. Such consequences could include a simple 20 push-ups for minor infractions or extensive yard work if the infraction warranted. Sending a child to their room is not an effective consequence and you don't want to associate going to their room as a punishment.

I had that responsibility to my children. Children find security in knowing where the boundaries lie and they need to trust them. They need to test their boundaries to know that they are still there so that they can trust them. For more on this topic read, James Dobson's *Dare to Discipline* or *Raising the Strong-Willed Child.* His wisdom on this topic is some of the very best. I urge you to read it if you have children.

Feed the Good Dog

I have always enjoyed the simple parable of the grandfather walking with his grandson, while the grandson explains to his grandfather how angry he is at someone. To which the grandfather describes that good and evil are two dogs that are constantly fighting within him. Surprised and intrigued, the grandson asks his grandfather with great interest, "Which one wins?" After a few more steps, the grandfather responds, "The one that I feed!" The parable clearly illustrates that we are the ultimate source of all of our actions. Which dog do you feed? Do you indulge your "right to revenge" and your justifications for being angry? Or do you feed the good dog, and always do the right thing even when others do not, especially when you don't feel like it? Do you feed on your emotions when deciding what actions to take or do you hold yourself to a higher standard than the standard of behavior you expect from others? Feeding the good dog requires that you diligently engage in activities that require your best, that help you hold yourself to your code of conduct and that you resist falling to the acceptable norm.

There is no shortage of resources for you to feed the good dog and starve the other. The very first book you should read is Proverbs in the Old Testament of the Bible. Proverbs is a collection of 30 lessons, instructions from King Solomon, son of David, to his son Lemuel, and a 31st lesson from his wife. Proverbs are the instructions of the richest and wisest man to walk the planet to his son. They are powerful, concise lessons on how to seek wisdom and understanding and avoid being a fool.

Music can also be an excellent tool to keep your mindset and perspective in the proper place. I particularly like old Motown music: it always does the trick. As a scoutmaster, I have the benefit of the Scout Slogan, 'Do a good turn daily'. When I do, it feeds the good dog. Working out and exercising, eating healthy also help you to feel good. When you feel good, it is easier to do good, but feelings aside, I urge you to do good, at all times. The point is there is no excuse for behaving like a boy when your wife and children need you to be a man.

The Golden Rule is another helpful reminder: "Do unto others as you would have them do unto you." Be forgiving and they may respond in kind.

The Good News About Turning 40

For many men, something happens when a man turns 40. He no longer has just a mental awareness of his own mortality. The physical reality that his life is half over begins to set in. When this occurs, a man begins to take stock of his life, his accomplishments and his regrets. If he hasn't given it much thought to this point, he begins to question what his time on this planet is all about. That timeless question of 'What is the meaning of life?' transforms to become personal and a man starts to question: What is the meaning of my life? What is my purpose? What am I going to do with the rest of my life, really?

For men who have made progress in this direction and for those whose focus has been predominantly serving others, this can be comforting and a reminder to stay the course and continue. Regrettably, for all too many men, there is a cold reality in this awakening, realizing that a significant portion of his life has been inwardly and selfishly focused. This will very likely leave a man feeling empty. From this point a man can go in two directions: he can ignore this tug of his conscience and fall deeper into himself, or he can break the chains of his selfish past by turning his focus outward and embracing his responsibility to others. While the latter may be desired, it can be difficult without the counsel and encouragement of other like-minded men.

In my *Boy Scout Handbook*, the Seventh Edition printed in 1971, as it describes what it means to be morally straight, it reads: "Your conscience speaks to you about yourself, about the moral obligation to make your life count." When a Scout hears and accepts this, it propels him forward, it makes him realize that he has something to contribute, that others count on him and that is WHY he must do his best. It continues on stating that Stradivarius, the famous Italian craftsman, is said to have said, "If I slack, I would rob God, for God can not make Stradivari violins without Stradivarius."

No one tells young men that they have a moral obligation to make their life count, *but we do*. You have a moral obligation to make your life count! So, do your very best!

Key Thoughts

- The only way to be a good father is to be a great husband.
- The less you need, the more you get!
- Job #1, take great care of your wife, your children's mother.
- Love is most certainly *still* a verb.
- There is no such thing as bad children, just bad parents.
- No man knows what his best really is, he only knows what his last best was.

Recommended Actions

- Lead by example.
- Pursue your wife and percolate her desire for you.
- The first and last kiss belongs to mom.
- Play the Game!
- Feed the good dog.
- Play music.
- Make your life count.

Questions for Reflection

1. Would you be proud if your son emulated your character and discipline? Would you be excited if your daughter brought home a man who was just like you?

2. Do you hold yourself to higher standards of behavior or do you use others' behavior as an excuse for your own?

3. What are you teaching your sons about how to care for a woman, by the quality of your care for their mother? What are you teaching your daughters about what they should expect from a man?

Chapter Five – Conflict, Divorce, and Restitution

"The easiest mess to clean up
is the one you don't make!"

What Happened?

No one enters marriage expecting it to fail. Unfortunately, very few couples enter marriage with the emotional self-discipline, training, support, or experience required to succeed. Good men fail every day because they don't know what they are doing and likewise don't understand how their well-intended actions can be negatively perceived by their wives. If you put an unlicensed driver behind the wheel of a Formula One race car, there is a very real likelihood, better than a 50% chance, that someone will get hurt, and badly.

This chapter provides more than a dozen insights to help you understand what may have caused, contributed to, or compounded the conflict in your marriage. Furthermore, it should help you understand what to do to restore your relationship. If you are willing to embrace these principles before you stumble into a conflict, you have an outstanding opportunity to prevent them in the first place. Remember, "The easiest mess to clean up is the one you don't make," so learn how to detect and avoid the landmines of relationship. Understanding and accepting the concepts that follow will save you the time, energy, and expense of a lot of cleaning up.

The Poor Woman is Just Trying to Have a Relationship with You!

I find it quite curious that men can be so quick to say how difficult their wife is, while thinking that they themselves are so easy to get along with. Think again! Let me remind you, your bad behavior stinks just as much as, if not more than, hers. In fact, your wife is more than likely behaving better than you are. Contributing to the conflict is the fact that men and women are in fact different. They see and perceive things differently. Things that are a big deal to you may be a little deal to her and things that are a little deal to you may be a BIG deal to her.

Understand that all too many women are also poorly prepared and equipped to be in a relationship with a man, so you must be tolerant. Their efforts to compete with men and be more masculine work against their need to be in a loving relationship. And the increasingly sexual environment often causes them to put more effort into their image instead of developing their natural beauty.

It is however more important to recognize and understand your own shortcomings instead of focusing on hers. Remember, Luke Chapter 6, Verse 42: "First remove the plank from your own eye, and then you will see clearly to remove the speck that is in your brother's eye." Recognizing your own personal quirks will cause you to be more considerate and accepting of her idiosyncrasies. Besides, this will give you something to do and that will help keep you out of trouble. You have 100% control over your behavior and just maybe a small influence on hers.

How Have You Neglected Your Wife?

If you are like most men, you went to great lengths to 'win the girl.' You wined her and dined her, perhaps you even took her to places that she liked that you didn't, just to get her to like you. Once married, it is natural for you to focus on the next unconquered pursuit and in the process neglect your wife or at a minimum take her for granted. This is extremely dangerous in marriage and often is the fast path to conflict.

Your wife wants to be important to you, and when you neglect her it communicates, again by your actions, that she is not important to you. There is a fundamental paradox at work that frustrates many men. She intellectually knows that she can't be the most important thing, lest she can control you. Yet emotionally, she desperately wants to be the most important thing to you. When I coach men, I tell them, *"Your wife knows that she is not the most important thing in your life, she just hates it when you remind her."* You must pay attention and be intentional in your efforts, using the five love languages, to let her know that she is important to you. In that way she will feel important and that will give her comfort.

Be Careful What YOU Look for You WILL Find It

In a similar vein, men and women have a bad habit of collecting evidence to support what they want to, or already do, believe. It turns out that our brains are even wired that way with something called the Ascending Reticular Activating System (ARAS) that searches for evidence of what we have already decided. Before I was awakened to this powerful insight, I used to look for and *find* fault in my wife. The natural outcome of this mindset is disappointment, conflict, and resentment. While the mechanism of the brain is highly complicated, I can direct it by deciding what I want to focus on. Now I look for reasons to be grateful for my wife and there are plenty. The natural outcome or consequence of this mindset is appreciation, generosity, and intimacy. My wife didn't change, I changed what I focused my attention on, and whatever I focus my attention on grows. Many of the things that irritated me before are still there, and all the things I now recognize and appreciate have always been there. I assure you, it is MUCH better now!

This is a powerful example of Max Planck's quote "When you change the way you look at things, the things you look at change."

Max Planck was a renowned German theoretical physicist who originated quantum theory, which won him the Nobel Prize for Physics in 1918. Transformation in a man's life occurs in the instant he changes how he sees himself in the world. This is the essential insight to eliminating conflict in your relationships.

It is also extremely important to recognize that when you are at the top of your game, feeling confident and secure in yourself, very little can throw you off track. I tease men by saying "when you're being that man at your very best, then she could burn down the house and you wouldn't care." While this is perhaps an exaggeration, you get the point. Likewise, when you are insecure, worried, and not confident in yourself or something else is unsettled elsewhere in your life, then all of your wife's behaviors that you have decided are annoying will manifest themselves in concert. So it is important to accept that many times she didn't do anything differently, you just responded differently. In those moments when you sense yourself being annoyed with her, you can ask yourself, "What's not going well in my life right now?"

Now I don't want to imply that I am perfect at this. It is something that requires vigilance, and every once in a while, when things are not going well with me, I stumble and my old behavior returns. Fortunately, I am reasonably adept at recognizing it when I stumble. When I do, I have a simple and very effective technique for getting myself back on track. When I notice that my attitude needs re-alignment, I will pick up ten things that are out of place and put them away. That usually does the trick. But when it doesn't, I do another 10 and somewhere by the fifteenth thing, I am back on track. I still follow through and complete the second ten. It is important that I follow through.

Men are physical creatures; having something physical that you can do to re-align yourself to being the man you expect yourself to be always helps!

Consciously Choose Your Attitude

Following up on the prior segment, everything that occurs in any given moment of our life is filtered and colored by our attitude or mindset. It is the most important aspect of yourself that you must master. The Oxford English Dictionary describes mindset as: "The established set of attitudes held by someone." Now we all have established sets of attitudes for our work, our marriage, our family, and at the root of all, our life. Our established attitudes become our default view and we adjust what happens to conform to that view. If your mindset is that your marriage is a burden, then you will interpret and search out evidence to support your attitude, and as a result you will perceive and experience your marriage as a burden. You must recognize what your default attitude is and then actively choose a new one, one that is positive and that will compel you to respond to conflict in the best possible manner. *What is your default attitude?* What are the consequences of holding that mindset? What attitude would you hold if you were being the best husband you could be?

Expectations and Conflict

Most conflicts arise from unmet expectations that you have of your wife, or that she has of you. Expectations are anything you think that she should or should not do. Often these are things you think that she should be doing for you. The Oxford English Dictionary defines expectation as: "a belief that someone will or should achieve something." When your expectations are unmet, they become a source of disagreement. Worse, you may start to believe that she is intentionally doing or not doing something that "she knows" you expect. When you do this, you take it personally and you convince yourself that you are being disrespected. Then you become resentful and your own behavior begins to deteriorate. *(More on this in a moment).*

Your wife may also have expectations of you, some reasonable and perhaps some unreasonable. Some may be based on how you treated her before you got married, when you were on your best behavior trying to "win the girl". Many expectations are a result of telling her that you would do something to win her approval or to avoid conflict that you then didn't do.

As for you, it is best if you do not have ANY expectations of your wife. Expectations are a way of trying to control your wife's behavior. And how do you react when you think that she's trying to control you? Pretty ugly, yes? You can make requests, but you don't get to whine if she doesn't do it and you must be appreciative if she does. If you can keep this mindset, she will likely respond favorably. If you are fortunate, there are probably many things that your wife does for you.

In fact, I encourage you to find things, perhaps small at first, that she can do for you. Remember, love is giving without expectations. If you allow her to give to you, it provides her the opportunity to experience love the verb and her feelings of love toward you will follow. This reminds me of a friend of mine who had a bad habit of rejecting his wife's offers to make him breakfast. I strongly encouraged him to simply say yes and accept her gift. Now he often gets steak with his eggs in the morning and now their marriage is that much stronger as a result. A man can be independent to a fault, leaving very little, if any room, for his wife to give to him. Never reject her offers, accept whatever she offers you. If you reject her offer, she feels rejected. It is as if you are saying, "I don't need or want you," and after years of this she will eventually stop, leaving you wondering what happened.

Remember, if you expect something, then you rob her of the feeling of giving. If you treat her with care and compassion, it will lead you to be generous with her and modeling this behavior may lead her to do the same.

Four Natural Responses to Conflict

Research has observed four natural responses to conflict. These responses are all programmed reactions designed to defend yourself, either physically or emotionally. The first and most common response is to escalate. If she attacks you, you snap back with greater intensity and if you are not careful, this could become physical; beware. This is commonly known as the ***fight*** response.

The second natural response is to withdraw, either physically or emotionally. Trained not to fight with their wives, many men simply retreat and withdraw. This is also known as the ***flight*** response. Oddly enough, it is often in emotional and physical withdrawal that men are most vulnerable to and actively seek the company of another woman. Don't. (*More on this later*). Also, when combined with escalation, your behavior deteriorates into a pattern of passive aggressive reactions that leave your wife scarred and the marriage damaged.

The third natural response is ***invalidating*** the other person, your wife. This is the most destructive and hurtful of all responses. Instead of arguing the topic, you find yourself attacking who she is, her qualities, behaviors and character. If you resort to name calling, then you are using the third natural response. This response is perhaps the most emotionally damaging of all. If you are guilty of this, you must stop immediately! And it doesn't matter if she did it first. You must discipline yourself so that you are able to respond and lead your family.

The final response, ***reading negative intentions*** into what she says or does, or doesn't say or doesn't do. This response, while more subtle,

I find is the most interesting. It is the epitome of "taking things personally." If there was unresolved conflict in your last interaction, you enter your next interaction anticipating and prepared for the conflict to continue. Predisposed with this mindset, you look for evidence that she is prolonging the conflict and you do this by projecting (reading) negative motives in her actions or words. Your preemptive response serves to fuel and perpetuate the conflict – if not escalate it. What is funny, but not ha-ha funny, is that, either out of arrogance and pride, you falsely credit yourself with having the best of intentions, while at the very same time, you falsely project upon and accuse your spouse of negative intentions. I find this human behavior peculiar. If we are honest with ourselves, more often than not, quite the opposite is likely to be true.

Be careful what you look for, you will find it!

The remedy here is quite simple, although not always easy. Give her and others in your life for that matter, not yourself, the benefit of the doubt. Assume that your wife ALWAYS has the best possible intention in everything that she does, and while it may not appear obvious or logical from your perspective, assume that she wants to be with you. ***Ascribe to her the highest possible intentions.*** The premise is, "I'd rather be wrong and do the right thing, than be right and do the wrong thing!" Who knows, you could be wrong and she may be hurt and acting spiteful, but that's no excuse for you to retaliate with the same bad behavior. If you exhibit restraint in these moments, she will come around and make up for her temporary lapse and emotional behavior. On the other hand, if you act badly and pour gasoline on the fire, however justified you may feel, it will only give her evidence to blame you for the conflict. I prefer door number 1, don't you?

Weapons of Defense

The four natural responses to conflict are weapons that you use to defend yourself. Weapons wound. In the words of popular singer Cher in her hit *If I Could Turn Back Time*: "Words are like weapons that wound sometimes..." These weapons inflict pain and sometimes irreversible hurt and the wounds can fester for a lifetime. You can't put the genie back in the bottle, you can never unsay something you have said. There is no such thing as "taking it back". When I first recognized my response as using weapons, I asked myself, "Why would I ever use weapons against my wife?" The only natural conclusion to that question was that I must put these weapons down and vow to never use them ever again. While this was difficult at first, something very important began to emerge. In order to actually stop using these weapons, I had to accept that there was ***nothing to defend***! She can't hurt me without my permission. And therefore, I no longer needed these weapons to defend myself. Certainly, I make mistakes, but I am no longer defending my actions. More on this later!

Give Her Permission Not to Like You

When coaching men through conflicts in their marriages, I will ask the man, "Do you like yourself all of the time?" When men are honest with themselves, they will readily say with confidence, "Of course not!" You know that you can be difficult to deal with from time to time, prone to be selfish, immature, emotional, and to behave badly. To this I reply, "How can you expect your wife to do something that you can't do?" After looking at it from that perspective, it begins to sink in. It has to be okay that she doesn't like you all the time. After all, you don't!

In fact, giving her the freedom to not like your behavior will give her the freedom to discover again why she loves you. Once again, another important paradox emerges, what she loves about you is most often the same thing she doesn't like about you. My wife loves that I am steadfast in my resolve, unless it is something that she disagrees with, then I am stubborn. Accepting yourself, the good, the bad, and especially the ugly will develop your self-confidence and help keep you from defending yourself. This self-confidence will benefit you in all aspects of your life. It will also demonstrate that *your wife can't control you* by giving or by withholding her approval.

Using Logic is Defending Yourself

Much has been written about men's and women's relationship to logic. In "*Defending the Caveman*", the Caveman does a very funny routine about how "women are not constrained by logic" and the audience roars with an even mix of laughter from the men and groans from the women. He then counters, "women are constrained by logic" bringing an equally loud roar of protest from the very same women. What he suggests is that women use logic until it doesn't serve them any longer. Men on the other hand rely on and operate on the structure and surety of logic. This fundamental difference is a major source of conflict in many relationships and it can all be avoided.

Logic is an essential quality for a man to be effective in the physical world and productive in his career, but it has little value in the land of relationship.

While you may have begun to master the four natural responses to conflict detailed herein, pay attention. If you are using logic to explain, educate, persuade, convince, coerce, or justify why you are doing, or not doing something, then you are *still* defending yourself.

If you find the need to justify yourself, you are defending yourself. Stop! There is nothing to defend.

Don't Take Things Personally

One of the primary things that will lead you to defend yourself is when you take the negative things your wife says about you personally. Remember what you were taught in kindergarten? *'Sticks and stones will break my bones, but names will never hurt them!'* You must remember this in times of conflict. What she says about you doesn't make it true. When you take things personally, it will trigger your ego and then you will feel justified in defending yourself. Has this ever worked? This behavior only escalates the conflict. Stop! Keep your ego in check at all times, no matter what.

Now, if what she says rings true in some regard and you don't like that about yourself, then pay attention. Don't get angry and don't defend yourself. Instead, figure out what you need to do to make sure that it is no longer true. Engage in the necessary discipline to develop your character. If you are able to do this, this too will help you to become a better man. Think of this as a service that she provides for you.

Anger

Never argue with your wife! Ever! For so many reasons, the most obvious of which is that you will do or say something that you will regret later, something that once done can't be undone. Apologies may temporarily soothe the pain, but they don't heal the wound. And if you do apologize, you must make sure that you never do it again! Repeated apologies for the same behaviors are not apologies at all. Secondly, you must always treat your wife the way *your* wife deserves to be treated. You would never tolerate someone else treating her in an angry or spiteful manner, so you must not as well. Thirdly, you teach your children based on your own behavior, not by what you say, therefore leading by example. If you observe your children disrespecting your wife, it is because you taught them it is okay.

You must discipline yourself so that you don't lose control and let your anger take over. "I can't help it" is a lie. Anger is a surface level and territorial response. It is easily provoked when you feel hurt, offended, disrespected, or betrayed. As you may begin to recognize, it is triggered by your perception of another's actions and your perception is not always accurate. Even if your perception is accurate, using another's behavior as an excuse for your own bad behavior is equally childish. More often than we should, when unrestrained, we find ourselves taking our anger out on someone close to us, when they aren't even the source of the problem, but just the most convenient target of our hostility.

Anger covers up the deeper and real underlying emotion. Notice that the word anger is in danger and dangerous. Unbridled anger is dangerous. Anger is a very important emotion, but you must learn to master it. Anger often comes in two forms and you should know the difference. First, anger is a territorial response, a clue that you feel threatened and that you feel the need to protect yourself. The second form of anger is when you are compelled to protect someone else. The latter form of anger is the valuable one as you can discover the roots of your purpose there. Anger is a doorway to discovering your deepest concerns and can help you recognize what you should stand for. This form of anger can and should lead you to action. Except when you are at risk of physical harm, there is no real need to defend yourself. But pay attention to what is beneath the anger, the emotional hurt, grief, or sorrow.

Now, how do you learn to control your anger? Contrary to contemporary Anger Management thinking, suppressing anger is not managing anger. Anything that is suppressed will continue to pressurize and eventually explode causing even greater damage. Instead, men must learn to express their anger in a manner where they will not harm themselves or others. It is best expressed physically and alone with other men. If you get angry often, a punching bag may be a good investment. Physical release allows you to see what is underneath the anger.

Likewise, it is equally concerning if you never get angry. It could be a sign that you are overly passive, emotionally detached, or resigned. Anger, when properly channeled, can and should be a powerful motivator that can be used to fuel your initiative and action.

Love and Respect

Dr. Emerson and Sarah Eggerichs describe another natural behavior men and women exhibit during conflict in their book entitled: *The Language of Love and Respect: Cracking the Communication Code with Your Mate.* Their research revealed that during conflict, women feel unloved and men feel disrespected. This hits at the heart of their primary needs: a man's need for respect that is rooted in his primary compass of honor and a woman's need for love that is rooted in her compass of relationship. Emerson writes: "Though we all need love and respect equally, the felt need differs during conflict. For example, when a woman feels unloved during conflict, her natural reaction is to respond disrespectfully. And when a husband feels disrespected during conflict, his reaction is to respond unlovingly."

Emerson appropriately refers to this as the "Crazy Cycle." "Without love a wife reacts without respect, and without respect a husband reacts without love." Then the relationship spirals downward, out of control into conflict. The adults start acting like children, while expecting their children to act like adults. But pay attention and notice that the seeds of conflict are watered by *your* feelings, which are rooted in your perception and expectations. It is easy to project negative intentions on and ascribe hurtful motives to your wife's actions or inactions and then use that to justify your own spiteful reaction.

Given these natural responses, you can see how a seemingly innocent comment can quickly spiral downward into a major conflict. In my seminar on Five Keys to Eliminating Conflict in Your Relationships with Women, I tell the men:

90% of conflicts didn't exist until you opened your mouth!

That's not an instruction for men to be silent, but for us to be responsible for what and how we communicate. And yes, don't defend yourself.

The key is to meet your wife's primary need to feel loved in every interaction and, most importantly, during conflict when it is against your nature to do so. This timeless command is clearly stated in Ephesians 5:33: "Nevertheless let each one of you in particular so love his own wife as himself, and let the wife see that she respects her husband." This gift of your love motivates her respect. Lead by being willing to go first, give love and the respect will follow. How you care for your wife reveals more about your character than hers. She is your wife, so be nice to her!

Be Responsible

Stephen Covey, author of *The 7 Habits of Highly Successful People*, highlights the difference between ***reacting*** and ***responding.*** Once in a relationship, it is common for men and women to develop a set of automatic behaviors or reactions to common situations, particularly during difficult times of conflict. For example, if your wife does or says something that you don't like and that triggers an immediate instinctual negative reaction, you are reacting. In the presence of this external stimulus, you predictably react in the same seemingly uncontrolled way. You do what you always do and you may even find yourself blaming your wife for your behavior. Notice that if you have programmed yourself to react automatically, you are no longer in control. If you are not in control, then by definition you are 'out of control'. *A man should never be out of control, ever.*

Covey challenges us to respond based on who we are, our values, and our care for those around us. He demands that we remain in control. When something happens, we pause and proactively, intentionally, and deliberately choose our response. When you are able to do this, you are able to respond instead of react. Covey advocates that when you can do this, you are being *response-able*. You are able to respond rather than just react. In order to do this, you must discipline yourself to be objective. This is very difficult, particularly during a conflict. There is no good reason to fight with your wife, ever. Notice your reaction to the previous statement; it says a lot. You must be able to see the faults in your own behavior as clearly as you see any faults in your wife.

Don't Buy Your Own Excuses, Justifications, and Lies

When you find yourself in the midst of a conflict, you may notice that you start to get creative, making up excuses and rationalizations for moving on. As the relationship seems to deteriorate, you may begin saying to yourself: "We got married too young," "I should have married _____," "I don't care." "I deserve better.".

These justifications may sound different, but their roots are all the same. Your justifications typically involve relieving yourself of the responsibility that you have and placing blame elsewhere, mainly on your wife. She did x first, or didn't do y, etc. They sound quite childish and petty from an objective distance. These excuses, justifications, and lies are things you say to yourself so you don't have to do the hard things that your conscience is telling you that you must do. You think you have a "get out of jail free" card from the consequences of your actions because someone else, namely your wife, didn't do what you expected her to do. You try to convince yourself that you are somehow free from any obligation to do what you know you must do.

Remember, your wedding vows sounded something very similar to, if not: *"in sickness and in health ... till death do us part."* Your vows were not, *"I do ... until or unless she does something I don't approve of!"* It is how you respond that matters. It is honorable to uphold your promise.

When the excuses and justifications are not enough, then a man will resort to telling himself lies. He tells lies to distance himself from the responsibility to clean up the mess. One of the most common lies a man tells himself is, "I have done everything I can." It sounds very noble and you can get your friends to agree with you so that it is your wife, not you, who is the cause of the failed marriage. In my experience this is almost never true, that a man has done *everything* he could. What is true is the man has only done what he was willing to do, nothing more. It was over because he quit. This is when a mentor is most needed. You need someone who will uncover your lies, dispel your excuses, and challenge you to act honorably and help you to fulfill your wedding vows. You must also have the courage to allow him to push you past where your ego would convince you to quit on your own. Don't quit; don't give up; and don't think divorce is a solution.

Another popular, reliable lie is *"I can't."* It might be true that you don't want to, you may not feel like it, you don't know how, but it is hardly ever true that you can't! Don't buy your own lie. When a man accepts the lies that he tells himself, he compromises his very character as a man. It is when things are the most difficult in life that a man's true character emerges and the quality of his character counts the most.

How a man behaves in his marriage is the most accurate reflection of his character!

This is true because your marriage requires something of you. During times of conflict any benefits are often obscured, seemingly few if any and so far from reach that they can't be recognized.

If you didn't know deep down that you are responsible for your actions, there would be no need to rationalize, to blame others, or to lie. I have observed that the only men who say "I don't care" are those who ***do*** care. They are only trying to relieve themselves of the responsibility of doing what they know, deep down, they must do.

The men who truly don't care never say this because they don't have to lie to themselves!

Notice that if you are determining your actions based on your wife's behavior, then she is controlling you, which means that you are out of control. Get back in control by doing your physical exercise or discipline as discussed earlier.

Never Use Anyone Else's Actions as an Excuse for Your Own

Expanding on the prior principle, as a man you should never use anyone else's actions or inactions as an excuse for your own. Reread the segment on Be Responsible earlier in this chapter. You must actively and consciously choose to respond in a manner that is rooted in and reinforces your character and that reflects your values. This concept, ***"Never Use Anyone Else's Actions as an Excuse for Your Own,"*** is a cornerstone lesson by which I have raised my six children. While they were often tempted to dismiss it, they were never able to ignore the truth of this lesson. It is the same as two wrongs don't make a right.

Now being responsible can be particularly difficult when your wife is not being responsible. A necessary side note, if you perceive her as being illogical or irrational, that does not mean she is irresponsible. But in those rare cases when your wife may be being irresponsible, you can't use her bad behavior as an excuse for your own. It is especially important when she is out of control that you must be in control. A man must discipline himself to always be in control. A good friend of mine once said, "The only time a man is off duty is when he is walking his dog." To which I said, "I don't have a dog." Then he said, "You should get one!"

Don't Fall Prey to Other Women

I find it strange that when men are having difficulty in their marriage, they all too often turn to another woman for comfort and reassurance, instead *of reaching out to* other men for counsel and companionship. This is extremely dangerous. Instead, when you are struggling in your marriage, the only place to go is to another married man for some good counsel and perhaps a good swift kick in the back side if needed. If you're a good catch, other women will feed on your need for comfort and lure you into a new relationship before the old one is over and you will begin to convince yourself that this woman is somehow better than your current one. Getting married is not about finding the 'right' woman, it is about becoming the right man!

Be careful, don't go to a newly divorced man because the consequences of his actions haven't caught up with him and he will indulge your attitude that 'she is the problem.' If he helps you fail, it will only protect him because he can justify his failure in yours. A divorced man who has paid the price can be good counsel if he will tell you the truth of what it cost him, his wife, and his children; and I don't mean financially, which is always significant, but not the greatest price to be paid.

Pornography

According to the website *Fight the New Drug* in their article *How Porn Changes the Brain*, "Repeated consumption of porn causes the brain to literally rewire itself. It triggers the brain to pump out chemicals and form new nerve pathways, leading to profound and lasting changes in the brain." Viewing pornography activates the reward center which releases the chemicals that make you feel pleasure. About one such protein (DeltaFosB), the article warns: "If it accumulates due to chronic overconsumption, any of us can end up with the brain changes that lead to compulsion and cravings to use. In fact, the drive to overconsume when enticements are around is found throughout the animal kingdom."

Viewing pornography has long-lasting effect on the brain since "DeltaFosB sticks around in the brain for weeks or months, which is why porn consumers may feel strong cravings for porn long after they've stopped the habit." If you find yourself not doing things you should so you can view pornography, then you are addicted. Pay attention. The danger is that it is all around and so pervasively available that it takes conscious efforts to avoid it. Pornography is an escape, a substitute for the real world.

Lead Us Not Into Temptation: The Truth About Affairs

It is said that when a man has an affair it is physical and when a woman has an affair it is emotional. If your wife has an affair, you must ask yourself, "How have I neglected or rejected my wife?" If you had or are having an affair, you must ask yourself, "How could my perceived physical needs be more important than the needs of my wife and family?"

Regrettably, too many men, when their marriage sours, instead of facing the headwinds and saving their family, turn toward the arms, breasts, and emotional comfort of another woman. When a man has an affair, he often justifies it because he isn't getting it at home. Are your needs for sex greater than your children's needs for a loving family or your wife's need for a husband?

The paradox is "the less you need, the more you get." If you need sex, it becomes a way that you allow yourself to be controlled. If you are being the right man, living up to your fullest potential, serving your purpose, you will get plenty of affection.

Lastly, if you have had an affair, you should *think twice before you tell her.* Telling your wife only relieves you of the guilt and only hurts her. It shifts the burden to deal with it to your wife. She probably already knows anyway. If you must confess, confess it to another man who will hold it in confidence or to your priest. If she knows about it, then you must sincerely and with repentance ask for her forgiveness, which she may or may not give.

Love is Still a VERB!

Unfortunately, "I don't love you!" has become the socially acceptable excuse for divorce in our no-fault, nobody is responsible culture. During conflict, couples base their decision to separate on the feeling of love or more specifically the lack thereof. However, the feeling of love is the noun and it is the by-product of doing loving things, i.e. love the verb. If you are guilty of saying to your wife, "I don't love you," or anything that sounds something like that, then what you are really saying is, "I have stopped doing loving things for you, I have stopped taking care of you." There are many reasons for that, but in order to restore the *feeling of love,* you must first restore the *actions of love.* Love is giving without expectations, *any* expectations. If you can wean yourself from your expectations, from your perceived needs, it will change the quality of your marriage and change your life, all for the better.

Inter-Dependence

Like myself, many strong men are what I would call 'independent to a fault'. Independence is an essential and very positive virtue like all other strengths. But it can become over-developed and then destructive to your relationship with your wife. When we had young children, I thought I would help my wife by not needing anything from her. Left unchecked this grew into "I don't need anything from you and I am going to remind you that I don't need anything from you by rejecting your offers." To another man, this would be perfectly acceptable and there would be no problem, but a woman reads this as "I don't want anything from you" which means "I don't want you!"

After twelve years of my wife offering to do things for me and twelve years of me innocently rejecting her offers, what do you think happened? She stopped offering. It's a wonder that it took that long. Once this was pointed out to me, I couldn't believe the damage I had done by something I thought was so small. Little did I know! Of course, from a man's perspective, being self-sufficient is desirable. But, not only had I rejected her, I had denied her the ability to express her love, to be generous and to experience the feeling of love that flows from love the verb. Now I am reformed and when my wife offers to do something for me, I simply say "yes, please." In doing so, I am learning how to become interdependent which is the whole point of being married in the first place. Learning how to recognize and appreciate how your wife's best qualities balance with your strengths and compensate for your weaknesses is essential for a healthy marriage.

Resentment

Back in Chapter Two, we explored how many men are controlled by what their wives think of them, by their approval and acceptance or lack thereof. A natural and common tragic consequence of allowing yourself to be controlled by your wife is that you blame her for it. You blame her for you not being the man of the house, for giving in, giving up, for changing your behavior to win her acceptance rather than doing what you need to do. Over time, you will begin to inventory all of the things you did to get her approval and begin to resent her for it rather than accept responsibility for it.

Resentment is the cancer that kills marriages.

Left unchecked, it will fester and infect the marriage and blind you from seeing the good elements. You must recognize and cast out any resignation you may have.

Forgiveness and Acceptance

There are more than 30,000 books written on Forgiveness, but they can all be traced back to John 20:23: "If you forgive the sins of any, they are forgiven them, if you retain the sins of any, they are retained." One of the best definitions that I have heard for forgiveness is ***"forgoing your right to revenge."*** Many believe that if someone intentionally harms you, you are entitled to revenge, 'an eye for an eye'. Revenge is easy, it takes courage and compassion to forgive. Forgiveness leads to healing.

Eleanor Roosevelt is quoted as saying, "No one can hurt you without your permission." Viktor Frankl, author of *Man's Search for Meaning*, after being brutally experimented on while in a Nazi prison camp, advocates that "man's last true freedom is to choose your attitude in any situation." Viktor Frankl survived when so many died around him because he was able to master his own attitude and having done so he was able to discover a great purpose to live. Others have said, "It is not what people do to you that hurts you, it is how you respond."

Much has been written about the cancer that festers and grows in the unforgiving heart. Refusing to forgive only enslaves the one who won't forgive. Forgiveness is the only antidote to the cancer of resentment that could destroy your marriage. You must forgive. It is naïve to think you will forget. You won't and I don't advocate that you try. But you must forgive. Your willingness to do so, or not, says more about who you are than anything about what your wife has done. If you say that you can't, you are only saying that you are unwilling to. In Mathew 18:21-22, we are charged to forgive seventy times seven. This is obviously easy to say, but incredibly hard to do. Hopefully this next paragraph will provide you with a perspective that will make it easier.

Notice that it is your own reaction to read negative intentions in her actions that fuels the conflict. I ask you, "What if you didn't have a right to revenge?" Then what? What would you do? What is left, when you simply accept that your wife is just as inept and ill-qualified as you are. Can you recognize that she has done the best that she could under the circumstance, with you on the other side? Furthermore, she too has been trying to protect herself in some way. Then what? You are left with just accepting her as she is, with all her "perfect imperfections." Just as you, deep down, desire that she will accept you. This is a good time to lead, by going first; she will eventually follow.

The Request Translator

Perhaps the most valuable principle in this entire book is this magical, almost mystical tool I invented called the 'Request Translator'. As I was studying all these dynamics between men and women, the nature of conflict, and the ease at which a simple incident can rage out of control, I had a thought. At first it was a simple thought: "What's missing?" I thought of how women hate rejection and about how men when challenged are almost pre-conditioned to defend themselves. I thought about the power of being responsible for what I look for, and then in a divine stroke of momentary brilliance, the pieces fell into place and there it was: The Request Translator.

Here's how it works. Anytime you hear words coming out of your wife's mouth that sound like a complaint about you (I know it doesn't happen very often, but when it does!), you are NOT allowed to respond (thank you Stephen Covey) until you are able to translate her complaint into a request. Again, unless you are able to translate what sounds to you like a complaint about you, you are forbidden to do or say ANYTHING. You must *learn to decode your wife's message by translating her words into a request for something that she wants.* If you are able to do this, two very important complementary principles are put into motion.

First, you disarm the natural triggers that lead to defending yourself, using the weapons of defense against your wife, and creating a conflict that didn't exist until you opened your mouth. That alone is good. Second, and more importantly, even if you are not able to satisfy or fulfill her request at that moment, you will be naturally drawn to do so. Men are naturally wired that way; we are *designed by God to do good.* When you ask a man to do something, particularly when it sounds like he is the only one who can do it, it is hard for him to say no. Absent all other conflicting thoughts, your conscience will compel you to say yes. So, in an instant, what could have been the source of a prolonged conflict is magically transformed into you being drawn closer to her and generating first love the verb, which then manifests in love the noun.

A simple example might be: "*You're never home*!" Now, you may recognize that complaints commonly come in the form of definitive statements, and we've learned early "Never answer a statement!" So that should be your first key to get the Request Translator out and power it up. Sometimes it takes a little while to warm up. On the surface, the statement may very well be true, so any attempt to defend yourself with stacks of evidence and justifications would just be futile. It only fuels the conflict. But you already know that. You've tried it, perhaps repeatedly, and it never goes well. Instead, what might your wife be asking of you? What is her request? While there may be several forms, she is ultimately saying, "I want to be with you" or "Will you spend time with me?" or, "Am I important to you?" Notice how your entire demeanor changes in an instant! You feel desired. This feeds your ego instead of being attacked, which provokes it.

So, give her the benefit of the doubt. Remember:

I'd rather be wrong and do the right thing,
than be right and do the wrong thing.

The Taming of the Shrew

In the early 1590's, William Shakespeare wrote *The Taming of The Shrew*, the classic tale of a father's efforts to marry off his daughters to good suitors. As was the custom, the eldest daughter was to be married before the younger ones could be wed. This tale was captured in the classic 1967 film bearing the same name with Elizabeth Taylor and Richard Burton. In the movie, Miss Taylor plays the bitter eldest sister, Katherina Minola, known throughout the town as the Shrew. With another daughter behind her, Bianca, the father offers a large dowry to the man who marries his eldest daughter.

Along comes Petruchio, a would-be noble who, while initially motivated by the large dowry, begins his earnest efforts to court Katherina. But she will have no part in it. Instead of welcoming her suitor, she becomes increasingly scornful and belligerent. The more difficult she becomes, the more persistent his advances. He returns spite with compliments. What is important is he is so secure in himself that he is never swayed or discouraged by her efforts to push him away. He doesn't alter his intention or change his behavior because of how she responds. Eventually she comes around and surrenders into his care. In the closing scene, Katherina's admiration of her husband is priceless as she scorns the other wives for not honoring and respecting their husbands.

Though a fairy tale, and controversial when viewed through a modern-day lens, the story reflects an important reality about the dynamics between men and women. As the story unfolds, Katherina learns to trust her husband and finds comfort in the security that he provides. Deep down, every married woman needs a man that she can't control.

A woman finds her security in the depth of your self-discipline.

The more disciplined you become, the greater the security you provide, the more intimacy will emerge. This is complementary cause and effect and both parties benefit greatly.

Divorce and Remarriage

Men, this one might hurt so get ready. All too many men would like to think that their wife or ex-wife is the source of all their troubles and that life will be better with a new woman. This is not the case, because YOU are the common denominator in both relationships. Unless a man recognizes how HE contributed to the demise of his marriage, he is at risk of repeating the story. While your wife contributes to the situation, a husband's leadership can change everything.

If you divorce your wife and the mother of your children, only to marry another woman so that you can be happy, your life will become complicated very quickly. First, you will be putting your perceived need for happiness above your children's well-being. What does that say about you? Second, the children begin years of being passed back and forth from parent to parent. This continues well into adulthood when they must choose with whom they will spend the holidays. You should plan on spending many without them.

Furthermore, if you make efforts to have a peaceable relationship with your first wife which you must, it will emerge as a source of conflict with your second wife, a no-win situation. I have frequently witnessed second wives being jealous of the time the husband spends with his children from the first marriage.

Worse, you start acting like they're your children, instead of "our" children. Again, it is about you. If you are divorced, you must continue to treat your ex-wife with great care and respect. She is and always will be your children's mother and their relationship with her is critically important.

In the end the real victims are your children. Holidays and family functions become a constant reminder of the broken family, as the kids are forced to spend time with each parent separately instead of together. It gets more complicated as you or your ex-wife begin a new relationship. Eventually you will realize the pain you've caused your children, and I promise you when you do it will become a source of great grief and regret. You will make every effort to deny that this is true, but in the end, you can't escape this painful reality.

The best course of action is to take 100% responsibility for the situation and do the work, develop yourself, so that you become the best man, husband, and father you can be. Seek counsel in married men who have the courage *to lead you past where you quit on your own.*

An Attitude of Gratitude

As mentioned in Chapter One, your attitude is the lens through which you see your circumstances and everything in your life. This is especially true when you find yourself in the middle of a conflict. What is the foundation of your attitude? How would others say you are predisposed to see things? What is your default attitude? For some it is rooted in hopelessness and resignation and for others it is rooted in hope, faith, and optimism. How can you master your attitude so that you are responsible and lead your family to a better outcome?

The attitude that will consistently lead you and others to the best possible outcome is an Attitude of Gratitude. When you are able to recognize and appreciate your situation and see what others have done for you, you will be compelled to be generous and provide to others what others have done for you. You will be obligated by yourself to Pay it Forward!

Gratitude is the Seed of Generosity

This is a fundamental principle for life. Keeping this in mind helps you to maintain a healthy perception and positive attitude. Even in the midst of a difficult situation, you can realize that you are blessed beyond your understanding. This will enable you to be more compassionate and generous with those in your care regardless of how they are behaving.

During my last trip to West Point's annual *Scoutmasters' Council Camporee*, I noticed a profound and powerful shift in the attitude of the cadets. These fine young men and women have an opportunity to do an unprecedented number of push-ups and other strenuous activities. The cadets have a choice. If they perceive the push-ups as punishment or a burden imposed on them, then they would naturally respond negatively and resist them. Instead, they have recently adopted an attitude of "They are free, and they are fun!" It is amazing that they now find enjoyment in their push-ups. With this change they are truly strong, mentally and physically. The same cadets, the same activity, a completely different attitude and a completely different outcome. They have taught me an incredible lesson.

This doesn't come naturally or easily. It requires an attitude alignment mechanism or tool. In the 1965 movie *The Sound of Music*, Julie Andrews demonstrates how "... I simply remember my favorite things, and then I don't feel so bad," can keep your attitude pointed in the right direction. Pastor and author Charles Swindoll's son, Chuck, tells a story in which his father retreated to his office after he had an argument with his wife. Chuck was concerned so he went in to see what his father was doing. He found him writing and asked what his father was doing. Charles replied that he was adding to the list he kept ... of the things that he was grateful for about his wife. What a powerful tool and a more powerful lesson.

Gratitude requires conscious effort. Pay attention and inventory if you must, as Charles did, all the things that your wife does for you and your children. How much of what she does goes unnoticed by you? Focus on and encourage the good. Be grateful and you will find it easier to be generous.

Be Patient

It may have taken years or even decades for your relationship to derail. It is critical that you develop patience and give your wife and your relationship time to heal, as much time as it needs. It may take a year or more. In some cases, it may require less time depending on the severity of the situation, the depth of the prior hurt, and the graciousness of you and your wife. There is no formula here and you must not set a timeline or establish preconditions that limit your commitment to restore your family. There is no end date and setting one keeps you from being fully invested. You must do what Captain Cortez did in 1519 when he landed in Veracruz: *Burn the Ships*. Set your focus and resolve on success; there is no retreat. Artificially creating a deadline only provides you with a timeline for quitting.

While restoring your marriage may appear seemingly impossible, it is worth your commitment and resolve. It is up to you. It is far better to fail than to quit. Your children's, your wife's, and even your health, well-being, and future are worth it. If you succeed you will change the course of your family for generations to come.

Restitution

All men make mistakes, some out of ignorance and others out of arrogance, selfishness, or lack of self-control. That is not the issue; what is important is how a man responds when that happens. Many men simply give up. They move from one failed relationship into the next. They grant themselves a 'get out of jail free card' and dismiss the cost to their children as they put their perceived need for happiness above that of their family. Other men will have the courage to take responsibility and discover what they must do. The honorable thing for a man to do is to fix what he has broken, to restore the damage he has done, and to take care of what has been put under his care.

The measure of a man is his willingness to be responsible for that which he is not responsible.

If you find yourself using your wife's behavior as an excuse for your own, then you are not being responsible for your actions. A man should not hide behind the childish response of "she did it first."

Instead of giving up and quitting you must study, learn, and prepare yourself to repair what has been broken. Do whatever it takes, no matter what. *Every restored marriage strengthens all marriages and every failed marriage weakens all marriages*. Your actions will, like it or not, have a direct impact on your children and those around you. You can be a source of hope for others or you can provide them justification for their own failings. Which path will you take?

DON'T QUIT

When the marriage begins to fail, another lie men say to themselves in an effort to convince them that they are good fathers is "I will do anything for my children." These same men are often the ones who are *unwilling to do what is needed to restore their marriage* and preserve their family. Again, they are only willing to do what they want to do.

Regardless of what has transpired or how long your marriage has been off track, it is not over until you quit. If you master the principles and lessons contained within these pages and persevere, then there is hope, there is a chance. You miss all the shots that you don't take. If you quit, then you will certainly be right, it is over and the damage will be done and the consequences are set in motion like a boulder rolling down a hill, destroying everything in its path. And your conscience will always know deep down that ***you quit***. There was a line you were unwilling to cross, a sacrifice that you were unwilling to make. There was an excuse, a justification, or a lie that you made up in order to relieve yourself of your responsibilities to your wife and the promise that you made in your marriage vows. It is on you. The law can't relieve a man of his obligation.

Quitting is, and will always be, the easiest thing to do. And it can quickly become a habit. Each time you quit, you allow resignation to win over courage. You chip away at the character of the man you know you could be and threaten the hopes of your children. When you quit on your marriage, then you weaken the institution of marriage itself as others will use your failure as an excuse for their own. What you say is meaningless, if your actions don't align.

It is extremely difficult, perhaps impossible, to maintain this level of conviction on your own. To help you with this, find a man who will help teach you to be accountable for your actions, a man who will help you hold yourself to a higher standard. A man who will really go to the mat with you and not let you give up on yourself, your wife, and your children. Someone who will fight for your family, especially when your feelings are leading you to give up. A man who will help you be the man your wife needs you to be.

Finally, have faith and persevere against the forces that would have you quit. Quoting from 1 Corinthians 10:13, "No temptation has overtaken you except such as is common to man; but God is faithful, who will not allow you to be tempted beyond what you are able, but with the temptation will also make the way of escape, that you may be able to bear it."

Don't quit.

Key Thoughts

- NEVER argue with your wife.
- In case you've forgotten......love is a verb!
- We live in a society where the adults expect their children to act like adults while they act like children.
- It is easy to be nice to your wife when you are getting what you want. Can you be a generous compassionate man when you perceive her to be difficult?
- I'd rather be wrong and do the right thing, than be right and do the wrong thing.
- Never use the weapons of defense on your wife...there's nothing to defend.
- Be careful what you look for; you ***will*** find it!
- It only takes one to lead. Where are you leading your family?
- Gratitude is the seed of generosity.

Recommended Actions

- Forgive, 70 times 7.
- Have your actions answer the question, "Do you love me?"
- Be objective.
- *Never use anyone else's actions as an excuse for your own!*
- Treat your wife the way your wife deserves be treated.
- Use your Request Translator.
- Don't quit.
- Master your attitude.

Questions for Reflection

1. What justifications do you use to make arguing with your wife acceptable to you?

2. What are the five most important things that you must do to eliminate the conflict in your marriage?

3. What attitude or mindset must you consciously choose to eliminate the conflict in your marriage?

4. What is your wife asking of you in her complaints?

5. What must you be forgiven for?

Chapter Six – The Golden Years

"Like a fine wine,
marriage gets better with age."

The Empty Nest - Now What?

Finally freed of the daily demands and responsibilities for your children, you are once again back where you started, a couple. *Two* are once again *one*. You have spent what seems like a lifetime and simultaneously a blink of an eye focused on establishing your career, raising your family, paying for college, accumulating wealth, and preparing for retirement. Now what?

For those who've invested in each other along the way, this will be a welcomed and peaceful transition. You will have time to enjoy each other's company. If you haven't cared for each other to the best of your ability, it can be an awkward and potentially challenging experience at first. What can you do?

Celebrate How Far You've Come

As Harry Chapin sings in *"Let Time Go Lightly"*, *"Old friends mean much more to me than new ones, because they know where you are and know where you have been."* By this stage in your life, you will likely have spent more time with your wife than without her. Together, you have weathered the storms and enjoyed the highlights of marriage, child rearing, your careers, the economy, profound joys, new beginnings, sorrowful ends, deep hardships and, yes, life itself. She has stood by your side and put up with your quirks. It is time to celebrate what you have accomplished together and the life you've lived together.

She knows you, perhaps better than you know yourself. She has cared for you, observed you and knows you by your actions. Thank her for her patience, care and love. Take time to acknowledge your wife for all that you have done together.

Revisit the Twelve Stages of Intimacy and the Love Languages

Since love the noun, the feeling of love, follows the verb, the expression of love, it is a great time to elevate your care for your wife. Back in Chapter Four we examined how, from the very beginning you and your wife progressed through twelve stages of increasing intimacy. You can continue to enhance the intimacy in your marriage by exploring again each of the steps along the way. Remember and remind each other of how you met and revisit the joy of your beginning. Hold your wife's hand when you walk together and continue to percolate her desire for you with a gentle touch or a playful kiss throughout the day. Continue to give without expectations.

By now, you know well what makes your wife feel cared for. Continue to express your care for her using the Five Love Languages discussed in Chapter Three by spending time with her, acknowledging her, buying her gifts, doing things for her and with a caring touch. Continue to lead her with the depth of your care and appreciation. If your children can witness this love after all these years, it will provide them a powerful example of how they should be with their spouses. More importantly it will give them continued hope for their own relationships.

Create New Beginnings

While you were young everything was new: marriage, having and raising children, places to live, jobs, hobbies, vacations to go on, and interests to explore. There was much to talk about. At this stage in life, so much has been said that sometimes it seems there is nothing left to say. Since language is the vehicle of relationship for your wife, it is important to seek out new hobbies, new activities, and new adventures that you can share together and talk about. These new things will help to fuel the continued conversation and connection that you share with your wife.

Continue to be generous. Discover new ways to meet each other's love needs. Hopefully with less demands on your time, you will have more time with and for each other. It need not be complicated; simple walks and quiet dinners together will go a long way. Find hobbies and activities you can enjoy together. A friend of mine spent weeks taking his wife to diners across the state in search of the best breakfast. Get good at being generous.

Mentor Younger Men

Your experiences: the good, the bad, and even the ugly have prepared you to be a resource, advocate, and counselor to the young men around you. If you look closely, your experiences have taught you many things along the way. More importantly, you may have made some mistakes, some costly ones. These personal life experiences are infused with powerful lessons. With objectivity, they have taught you what you value and what is truly important in your life. It would be naïve to think these lessons were given to you for just your own benefit. You are to pass them along, so other men may benefit from the good and the bad of your experience. These are the critical lessons to pass along in an effort to protect other men and their families from the same tragedies, hardships, and heartbreak. While you may believe that it is too late for you, you may find peace and solace in knowing that you have helped save others from unnecessary hardships. Remember Robert Bly:

"A man will give his greatest gift to the world, through transcending his deepest pain."

What lessons has your life taught you? How can you use them to make life better for those who've come after you? Interestingly, actively helping others is the only sustainable way for you to keep yourself on the right path.

This book is my humble attempt to do just that: to offer to you and to your family the insights, tools, and understanding needed to create and sustain a healthy and thriving family. A marriage where everyone: you, your wife, and especially your children, experience the greatest love, security, and hope. This is the foundation on which your legacy lives. Helping men have great marriages, amazing families, and a fulfilled life gives me great joy. This is my sole desire for you.

Invest in the Marriage of Others

Regrettably, when a couple finds themselves in a little "hot water", nearly all of those who could help them don't. They hide behind a myriad of excuses: "I am not comfortable..., I don't want to interfere...", etc. I have even heard family members when speaking about their own family say, "It's none of my business." Nothing could be further from the truth. If you don't step up then who will? We've all been witnesses at weddings when the priest asks the congregation: "Will you who are present do *EVERYTHING* in your power to uphold these people in their marriage?" and without hesitation a gleeful reply is heard, "We will." But a few short years later, when that very same couple starts going off course, everyone reneges on their promise. They fail to fulfill their obligation to do everything in their power to uphold these people in their marriage.

A few years ago my eldest son got married. As the rehearsal dinner came to a close on the eve of his wedding, I gathered the groomsmen, the father of the bride, and all the men who were close to my son into a room. I reminded them of the promise that they would make the next day and charged them with the obligation to live up to that promise. It was a powerful and personal time among the men and it changes their context for their wedding. I have led others to do the same at their weddings. It is our responsibility now as older men to set an example and hold the standard.

When a couple fails, it is not just the couple who have failed, it is their family, their friends, and their community around them that have failed. Those who could have helped didn't or lacked the confidence, courage, or conviction to go far enough, to stand up for them when they couldn't stand for themselves. Are you willing to make a stand for another family? I often think of the motto, the context that the Coast Guard rescue divers use: "So that others may live!" Taking a stand doesn't put your life at risk, but it can save a man, a marriage, a family and in many cases save a life or two! Every time I hear of a domestic dispute that ends in murder, suicide, and all too often both, I grieve for the couple, the children, and their family. It didn't need to be. And while that is the most obvious, something very real dies within a child when his or her parents get divorced.

It is time to use your gifts that life has given to you to strengthen other men and their families. If you don't, these men may crash on the same rocks of deceptive lies that you bought from yourself. However, if you invest in other men, you may be the difference another family needs to survive. When you do this, it will bring some peace to yourself. Breathe life into other men's lives and in doing so, bring new life to your own.

If are unwilling to stand for someone else's marriage, it will be increasingly difficult for you to stand for your own. More importantly, it is the very act of investing in others that compels me to live up to my counsel at home. Finally, if you are unwilling to make a stand for another, what right do you have to expect others to help when you need it or when your children need it?

Loss and Regrets

The good news about turning forty years old is that you have the physical experience that your life is nearly half over. By the time you reach sixty, you have consumed your most productive years and there is a long enough wake behind you for you to gauge how you are doing. At this point, aging is no longer a theoretical concept; it is ever present in your physical experience. You just don't move as you once did and gravity has begun to take its toll. The reality of your own mortality should help you to remain focused on what is important in your life and what still lies ahead. Some dreams and aspirations may now be lost, while many others remain attainable with dedication and perseverance, but the effort must accelerate. So, it is time to double down with conviction and action. If there is anything left undone, now's the time to take action.

The Merriam-Webster dictionary defines "regret" as: "to mourn the loss of." Aside from losing people close to you by death, a man should live his life in a way that he has no regrets about how he has lived his life. Unfortunately, most men do have regrets. Regret is not bad, if you pay attention to it and soon enough to do something about it. Regret reminds you what you care about. Sincere regret leads you to repent. If it is something you left undone, now is the time to do it.

As you objectively reflect on how you lived your life, you may uncover times when your actions caused others hardship, pain, or suffering. You may have severed an important relationship, cheated on your wife, or worse. Make a list of your regrets. First, list all the things that you have left undone, and **write what actions you will now take and by when.** Next, list all the things that you have done that you ought not to have done and repent. Make a plan to remediate, restore, or resolve each regret. In this way you can clear the burden of these regrets as you begin to make the most of your remaining time.

Meaning, Purpose and Legacy

Women hold within themselves the power to create life, to give birth. Men can't do that. That fact leads men to find meaning in their purpose and legacy, in what they accomplish, measured by what their contribution is. Thus, men are driven to create, compete, and conquer things. Men build things and blow things up. That's it, pretty simple. We create companies, bridges, and buildings. We conquer mountains, quests, and similar challenges because they are there and to see if we can. Every man has a legacy; I charge you to be responsible for the quality of that legacy. Is and has your life been about you, your perceived needs and selfish desires?

Have you dedicated yourself to fulfilling your obligation to make your life count?

As you mature, the question of what is the meaning and purpose becomes increasingly prevalent in your awareness. For men who answered this question and honorably served, the fruits of their efforts become a source of comfort. On the other hand, this can be very troubling for men who've carefully avoided the question and evaded the responsibility to contribute to others in a meaningful way. It is even worse for those who now realize the price others have paid for their selfish behavior.

Retirement

Isn't it odd that so many men spend their lifetime looking towards their retirement? Now I hope you have planned and prepared along the way so that you have the financial ability to retire. If not, you may not have any option but to continue to work or severely limit your lifestyle. It is now that the financial cost of divorce becomes all too painfully obvious. Retirement from work does mean more time for other things. But what?

You may retire from a job, but you can't retire from your purpose. If you have led your life guided by your purpose, by the time you are of an age to retire, you will find yourself having finally achieved the wisdom to serve this purpose well. You will be drawn to continue and you should, lest the lessons of your life be lost. If you haven't guided your life by your chosen purpose, now is the time to create the legacy defined by the obituary you would aspire to have written about you.

Key Thoughts

- The only way to care for your children is to care for the community that you will leave for them.
- If you don't, who will?
- Don't expect anything from someone else that you are not willing to do yourself.

Recommended Actions

- Rekindle the romance.
- Celebrate your marriage.
- Create new beginnings.
- Mentor younger men! Invest in them.
- Make your life count.

Questions for Reflection

1. How will you use the lessons that your life has taught you to make life better for others?

2. What new activities and adventures will you begin with your wife?

3. What is the legacy of your life?

4. What is left undone and what is next?

Chapter Seven – What Men Should Know About Women

"They are MUCH better at this than we are."

Recap

While I have touched on many of these individual topics in the preceding chapters, it is good to take a second look at them, collectively, so you can see how they are interrelated and you will notice the combined effect of these insights and behaviors.

Women are Emotional!

Any attempt to change her behavior would be futile and be akin to trying to get her to act like you, like a man ... and you won't really like it when she starts acting like one. Give her the freedom to have her emotions, but don't allow yourself to be consumed or controlled by them.

Do not hook your emotions to her emotional rollercoaster!

Just because she gets emotional, that doesn't give you the right to get emotional in return. That's childish. Instead find your well-being in your commitment to your purpose and the respect of other men. Just as a ship at sea in turbulent waters gains stability through forward motion, so should your life's purpose provide you stability as you navigate the challenging waters of life. Remember, her security is rooted in the depth of your self-discipline.

Her Objective

A woman's objective is to land the best man she can, and by best man I mean the man who is best suited to take care of her and her children, to provide for and protect them against any threat, no matter what! Biologically, a woman needs a man to protect her from harm while rearing her children. Regrettably, this is not so obvious in today's relatively 'secure' environment of a world superpower where the risks to her survival are greatly subdued. Protected by cultural norms and laws, many women try to deny their need for security and overcompensate for it by trying to prove themselves in masculine arenas. Some women even try to prove to themselves that they don't need a man and use that to lessen their interest in a relationship. They exhibit masculine, aggressive, and competitive qualities that are not very attractive nor well-suited for nurturing the emotional well-being of a child. This prevailing attitude and behavior devalues a woman's natural gifts and robs her of her best qualities. Increasingly, women may earn more than their husbands, leading them to think they don't need a man, except for an occasional plaything.

A woman needs a man's man, a man who has the respect of other men, because that will provide him, and therefore her, access to resources. This is a man who is certainly not controlled by what other men think of him and a man who is certainly not controlled by women. This is a man who will provide her security which most often translates to financial security.

For better or worse, ***you*** are the best man your wife could get. And don't flatter yourself by thinking you're something special. Make her look good by being the best man you can be, always. Hold yourself to the highest possible standards regardless of what others may do! Care for your wife, in a manner that reflects your character, in a manner that your wife deserves.

Your Mission

Your job is to be the very BEST man you can be so that you fulfill your obligation to make your life count. Now this may sound trite, but it is true. Since her job is to get the best man she can, the ONLY thing you can do now to make her successful, since she already has you, is to challenge yourself to become the best man you can be. Your job is to provide for and protect your wife and your children, to subordinate your self-indulgent desires to ensure they are safe and secure. Your care and commitment should expand outside your home and include taking care of the world that you will leave your children and your children's children in. A man who willingly accepts this responsibility will be successful because the needs of those whom he cares for require him to be a better man. This requires and causes you to develop self-control, which is just another way of saying self-discipline.

So be the best man you can be, at all times and in all ways. In the words of Patriots' Coach Bill Belichik, "Do your job!"

A Woman's Greatest Fear

A woman's greatest fear is being abandoned or rejected. I have witnessed women who are insecure in their marriage subconsciously push their husbands away to protect themselves from being hurt. While this makes no sense to a man, the paradox is that she is trying to see if you are really committed. You must be steadfast in your resolve no matter what your wife says or does. You alone must be the master of your actions, rooted in the legacy you intend to create for you and your family. Always lead, get help, and never quit! If you are disciplined and steadfast, your wife can relax, knowing that you won't hurt her by leaving. Then she will reveal the depth of her true love to you.

Language

For men language is the vehicle of communication, of instruction and information; for women language is the vehicle of relationship. A man speaks to convey information and in turn he listens for the important information in the words of others. The words are what he intends to communicate. Women speak to make a connection, to establish a relationship. The words enable the relationship. Ever notice that when two women meet who haven't seen each other in a while, they seem to have three conversations simultaneously?

This drives a man nuts because a man wants to know what the point is. In many cases there is no point, except that she wants to have a relationship with you, HELLO! Alison Armstrong, author of *Celebrating Men, Satisfying Women*, in her seminar, does an amusing routine in 'How Women Speak – Part II: Life Threatening Details.' She describes, when picking berries, the critical importance of identifying safely edible berries as distinct from the dangerous, poisonous ones. Then she distinguishes between 'Berry Markers' and 'Berry Markings.' She explains that Berry Markers are the words a woman uses to describe time and place, and where and when. Berry Markings, on the other hand, are the words a woman uses to describe the distinguishing and painstaking details of what she's talking about. Armstrong says that a man must learn the difference between the two and that in many cases there is no point, except for what is most important to her ... a relationship with *you*. Her YouTube videos are well worth taking a look at; there is truth in her humor.

My wife often asks me to talk to her, but often she has nothing in particular that she wants to talk about. While I find this annoying from time to time, it is very important that I remember she wants to be connected to and important to me. Therefore, I strive to cooperate with her and have something to talk about. She is only seeking the attention and connection in the relationship that she derives from verbal communication.

So it is very important that you learn how to listen for the actual communication instead of just the words that you hear. What is the message that lies between the words? What is the request that she is making and how can you respond to this request? Go back and revisit **The Request Translator** in Chapter Four - it is truly priceless. Be alert, if you listen your wife will give you some very valuable information in the midst of the less interesting details.

Furthermore, a woman will often say something to see if it fits, to see if she believes it. This causes men great angst, because we assume that she meant what she said and we respond accordingly. A man doesn't do that, he says what he believes (except when he's telling himself a lie). In Adele's pop hit *'Rumor Has It,' she sings: "Just because I said it, doesn't mean I meant it*." You need to learn to distinguish between temporary emotionally-charged feelings and what is true. Resist your tendency to respond to the former.

Multi-sensory Perception

Women rely more heavily on their emotional senses than men do. In relationships with men, women have a built-in lie detector. A woman will listen to what a man says and then see if what she hears lines up with what she senses from the man's actions. If your actions match your words, then she's more likely to trust the you. If your actions conflict with what you say, then she won't or shouldn't trust you. Unfortunately, some women ignore their natural intuition, wanting to believe what they hear from the man, and they often wind up getting hurt in the end. For a man to provide his wife security she must be able to trust him.

It's Always About Her

Being relationship-centric, women are very concerned about what other people think of them and how other people's opinions of *you* also reflect on *them*. This will cause her to be critical of any of your behaviors that will cause others to think less of *her*. I can't count how many times Nancy has said, "Behave", when prepping me to meet new people. As if to say, 'don't be yourself.' If I was prone to defend myself this could easily start a conflict; instead I just relax and make a joke about it.

Resist her efforts to have you conform. It is another way you might be tempted to let her control you. Remember, if she can control you, other women can control you, which puts her relationship with you at risk.

Conversely, if you act honorably and it garners you the respect of other men, it will make you attractive to her, percolating her desire for you and drawing her towards you. Be a man that other men count on and respect.

Guided by the Compass of Relationship

A woman's central navigational system is relationship. Her strength lies in her emotions and her natural instincts to care for and protect those she loves. She wants everyone to be happy and to like her. When women lack the security provided by a committed relationship with a man, they are forced to exhibit masculine traits to provide and protect themselves which in turn compromises and inhibits their nature. Competition and cooperation are opposing objectives. The goal of competition is to win at the expense of others who will lose; the goal of cooperation is mutual shared benefit. Competition erodes relationship, cooperation enables relationship. Don't compete with your wife in any way. Even when playing friendly games you must be certain not to get your ego engaged and become overly competitive. Can your ego allow her to win?

Low Self-Esteem

Rooted in their primal fear of being abandoned, women are insecure and they hate rejection. Instead of asking you to do something and risk being rejected, you may notice that she will say "We need to do...," so pay attention. This is her way of asking you for something. An astute man will take the hint and take care of her needs if he is able to. You can also uncover what she thinks she needs by listening to what she complains about. If you didn't make the connection, go back and re-read **The Request Translator in Chapter Five** and then, read it again!

Also, I have discovered over the years, Nancy's self-esteem has grown, fueled by the depth of my love and care for her. It is a wonderful and generous gift to give to your wife and your family.

The Illusion of Control

As I mentioned earlier, a good man provides his wife security. Every woman needs a man that she can't control; the only way for her to know if she can control you is to try. So ironically, a woman feels more secure when she is with a man that she can't control. If a woman can control her man, then other women, particularly those who she perceives are better than she is in some regard (younger, prettier, more attractive, nicer), can control her man as well. If you can be controlled by a woman, then she is not secure in her relationship with you.

Furthermore, she won't respect a man that she can control. If a woman can control her husband, she is worse off with him than without him. If your wife is insecure in her relationship with you, you will never receive the depth of the love that lives within her. She will keep her guard up in an effort to protect herself from being hurt when you leave her. Sadly, there is no shortage of examples of men who leave their wife for another woman, which further fuels their insecurity.

The most important thing that you provide your wife is security. Security that is rooted in your ability to control yourself in all aspects of your life, and your ability to do what you must do, regardless of how hard it is or how you might feel about it.

Your wife finds her security in the depth of your self-discipline.

Make certain that she feels safe and secure.

Sex

Regrettably, sex has been, is, and likely will always be the easiest way for a woman to control a man. Women know this from a very young age and today's media only serves to reinforce this fact with a constant barrage of sexually charged advertising, programming, and electronic media. There exists, at a fundamental level, a dirty trade between men and women: Women trade sex for intimacy and men trade intimacy for sex. This is elaborated on more eloquently in *What Women Want: What Every Man Needs to Know About Sex, Romance, Passion, and Pleasure* by Laurence Roy Stains and Stefan Bechtel.

In casual relationships, this is a dangerous and costly exchange. This dynamic only fuels a woman's lack of self-esteem as they know that sex is abundantly available. Despite her efforts to trick her mind to the contrary, women know instinctively that the man is mostly with her for the sex. The more insecure a woman is, the more promiscuous she becomes, which only fuels her insecurity. Old wives' tales are old wives' tales for a reason: they are generally true. It is a way to pass down tribal knowledge from one generation to the next. The relevant one for this topic is, *"If you give him the milk, he won't buy the cow!"*

Furthermore, once a woman has sex with a man, she knows that her ability to keep him will diminish over time, particularly as she ages. If a woman has a good man, she is always at risk that another woman will take her man away.

Science is revealing that during sex both men and women release a hormone, oxytocin, that causes men and women to bond. Oxytocin is released in high quantities at three times for a woman: when a woman gives birth, when she breast feeds her baby, and during sexual arousal and release. For men it occurs after intercourse. Studies have shown that oxytocin enables bonding and increases the attractiveness of the partner compared to the attractiveness of other females, revealing a biological factor behind monogamy.

Prolonged promiscuity wounds a woman's ability to be intimate, which you might expect, but it is true for men as well. Having multiple partners ultimately inhibits your ability to be bonded with your wife.

Living Together

Contrary to what women think, cohabitation does not lead to a successful marriage. It does, however, often lead to unplanned pregnancies, prolonged uncommitted relationships that end after five or worse, ten years, or marriage by default. None of these are desirable outcomes and the woman bears the greater cost in all of them. Cohabitation provides the man the superficial benefits of sex absent the commitment that drives him to be a better man. And what does the woman actually think she will get in return? Women, if a man isn't willing to marry you, you shouldn't live with him! What makes you think he'll change his mind later? Living together isn't something that should be taken lightly or to be tried out like test-driving a car. I've seen far too many couples move in together thinking they are different and they know what's best, only to separate years later. Since men struggle ending relationships, there is a real risk that you will go along and get married to appease her, which may not be the best choice.

I tell young men that they should never marry a woman who would live with them before they got married or at least engaged! It reveals her lack of self-confidence. If she is worth marrying, she is worth your commitment. If not, move on.

Responsibility

Women hate to be responsible. Given the option, a woman will try to make <u>you</u> responsible for a situation, particularly a negative one. You need to read a lot of John Gray to filter out the gems, but one thing he suggests is that women try on emotions like they try on clothes: to see if they fit! Translation, women don't always mean what the words they are saying mean literally. A man generally means what he says. So, we listen to the words and respond to the words. This difference often frustrates men causing unnecessary conflict, particularly when a man does what his wife said, but it's not what she wanted. If things aren't going well in your relationship and she says, "maybe we should get a divorce…" and you respond by calling the lawyer, then *you* are responsible for the divorce. Women will say something to see if it fits or as a test to see what you think. If you leave, if you quit, then you will be responsible for tearing your family apart. Women need to know where you stand and what you stand for. Be responsible, don't quit, even if you think she wants you to.

Her Career

According to the US Census, both parents work in 61% of the homes with children under the age of 18. Given the cost of living this is almost inevitable. However, the male-oriented, competitive corporate environment can be toxic to a woman's natural abilities. It forces a woman to cultivate and exhibit competitive masculine qualities in order to succeed. This moves her away from the natural loving and nurturing qualities that are her primary feminine qualities. Furthermore, if your wife is financially independent, this can keep her from counting on you and from creating a deeper level of trust and intimacy in your marriage. Many wives are and will continue to be in these roles and you must understand the consequences to your relationship if she works in this arena.

There are many traditionally female professions like teaching, nursing or other service-based roles that provide a woman the opportunity to use her best qualities in caring for others. It is not that I think women should not be engineers, construction workers, or executives; they are more than capable. However, the more competitive the environment, the more you need to recognize the consequences. Women are being unduly encouraged to put their work before their families and all too often the few women who are able and choose to suspend their career to raise their children, are chastised by their peers.

She Treats You Like a Woman

You are not your wife's girlfriend so stop trying to be one. Similar to men treating their woman like a man, women struggle with the same thing. They often treat their man like a woman, and they go so far as to try to get you to behave like one. They think that you would be 'better' if you acted like she does. Left unchecked, you may start acting like one and once you do, you are of no value to her. Your woman needs you to provide the security that accompanies a disciplined, masculine, competitive presence.

This is a primary reason that young men need fathers to balance out the mother's influence. ***A mother's job is to make sure the son doesn't get hurt. A father's job is to make sure that he doesn't get hurt too much.*** Somewhat ironically, most women wouldn't marry the sons they are raising because they are raising "good little boys," compliant and safe, not men of courage, character, and conviction who will persevere through adversity instead of cowering in fear.

Make Sure She Spends Time with Other GOOD Women

Just like you, it is critical that your wife spend time with other good women. Not only will she receive good counsel from them, equally important she will be inclined to offer sound counsel to them. Just as with you, if she is extending help to other women, this will work to keep *her* on track. The counsel she gives to other women, she will likely follow for herself and be reminded what works in her relationships. This is good for her, which is very good for you. When women have strong relationships with other women, it satisfies a relationship need that you can't nor should you try to fill. She will return 'filled' by her ladies. As with a man, a woman will regain a more objective perspective about her own circumstances or troubles when she recognizes the challenges that another woman is facing are more difficult and pressing than her own.

Love and Control

Women have two opposing relationship management styles: Love and Control. When a woman is secure in her relationship and confident in her abilities, she will engage in *all* her relationships in a loving and generous manner. This is what men find most attractive. When she is insecure, she will revert to control. This, on the other hand, is not so desirable. While you may have no direct control over her behavior, you have a great influence on how secure she feels in the relationship. So instead of criticizing and complaining when she is controlling, seek out ways in which you can make her feel secure. If you consistently communicate with your actions that you will always care for, provide and protect her, then you will experience greater love from her.

Women in Love Glow

Ever notice that women who are pregnant have a very attractive glow about them? Their spirit is renewed and full of life. They are filled with the love and joy that accompanies new birth. However, a woman doesn't need to be pregnant to glow, to be full of life and full of love. A woman's glow is rooted in the natural love that is within her. This is extremely attractive to a man. When a woman is centered in the love that is her inner best quality, she is radiant and she draws men toward her. Your role in this is to create an environment where she is safe, secure, and taken care of. This will enable her to relax, surrender into your care and provide her with the confidence to be herself.

Key Thoughts

- For women, language is the vehicle of relationship.
- Are you strong enough to be her man?
- The longer she is talking the less you are listening!
- Your wife finds her security in the depth of your self-discipline.

Recommended Actions

- Master your emotions.
- Treat her like a lady.
- Listen, listen, and listen again.
- Be honorable.
- Encourage her to spend time with other women.
- Have things to talk about.

Questions for Reflection

1. What quality must you develop in your character to be the best husband and father you can be?

2. What will you do to make your wife feel secure in the marriage?

3. In what ways do you treat your wife like a man? What will you do instead?

Chapter Eight – Conclusion

"Your words mean nothing;
your actions say everything!"

Leadership in Action

At the end of the day it all comes down to your ability to lead yourself and then your ability to lead your family based on your actions. The direction of your leadership comes from the foundation of your life, your purpose. Your purpose will determine the qualities of character that you must develop. You must consciously choose and master the attitude necessary to sustain the self-discipline required to navigate the storms of life so that you can serve your purpose.

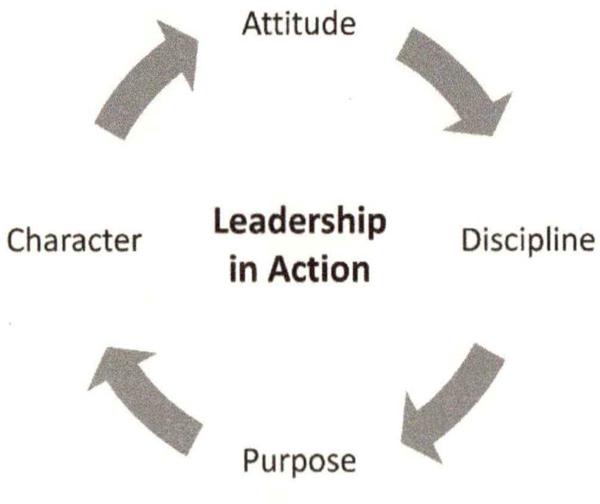

If you focus on these four attributes of your life and remain true to your values, you will create an amazing legacy for yourself, your wife, your children, and your community.

An Honorable and Worthy Journey

As I mentioned at the beginning, getting married and becoming a father are two of the most important rites of passage in a man's life. When served honorably and well, they will help transform you from being a boy, focused on your own selfish desires and perceived needs, to a man who honorably cares for and serves the needs of his wife, his children, and his community. Equipped with the proper mindset, the obligations and responsibilities that accompany these roles will cause you to become far more disciplined than you would ever be on your own. Your responsibilities make you better *because* they require something of you, because they pull you past where you would quit on your own. The resulting self-discipline will fuel your success personally and professionally, thereby enhancing your accomplishments, contributions, and the very meaning of your life.

The consequences of neglecting this challenge are severe. Absent the tug of responsibility from those who count on you, you will be tempted to settle for 'good.' You will give in to, and give credibility to, your feelings about what you like or want to do. You will be prone to excessive procrastination and you will fail to do many of the things that require something of you. But is good, good enough for you? Remember, good is the enemy of great! And good enough is never really good enough. Settling for anything less than your best could lead to a life of emptiness, insecurity, loneliness, addiction, and in the end regret.

Men's Brains and Women's Brains are Different by Design

In her book, *The Male Brain: A Breakthrough Understanding of How Men and Boys Think,* author Dr. Louann Brizendine reveals that the part of the brain that controls sexual pursuit deep inside the hypothalamus is 2.5 times larger in a male brain than a female brain due to the effect of testosterone and our Y chromosome. This creates in men a 300 percent greater interest than women in sex at every age. There is growing neurological research that explains what we've known all along, but our increasingly feminine-oriented culture is trying to ignore.

"Men also have larger brain centers for muscular action and aggression. His brain circuits for mate protection and territorial defense are hormonally primed for action starting at puberty. Pecking order and hierarchy matter more deeply to men than most women realize. Men also have larger processors in the core of the most primitive area of the brain, which registers fear and triggers protective aggression -- the amygdala."

The outer layer of the brain, the cortex, controls most of our thinking. In men, the right side of the cortex controls spatial thinking. This is science that the current American Psychology Association is trying to ignore, advocating that masculinity is somehow toxic. What is a young man, or even a grown man for that matter, to think when he is told by the media and educational system that everything that is traditionally male (competition, aggression, etc.) is bad, and at the same time that girls can and should do anything a man can do even better? Especially when that includes girls exhibiting the same masculine qualities that the boys are being told that they should suppress. And we wonder why we are losing a generation of men to doubt and addictions!

We would best be served by recognizing and valuing the biological differences that make men male and women female. We need to stop trying to emasculate men while endeavoring to train women to be men.

Self-Discipline

Fifty percent of leadership is leading yourself. The essential key to living a fulfilled life depends on your ability to discipline and lead yourself. Are you able to do the right thing, not when it is easy, but when it is difficult and when it requires something of you? Are you able to follow through when it requires a real sacrifice or puts your security at risk in some way? As you already know, it is far easier to stay physically fit once you are in shape. However, getting in shape requires a great deal of effort when you are not. Are you in shape mentally, physically, spiritually and emotionally? If not, it's time to get in shape. If yes, raise the bar and hold yourself to a higher, more demanding standard.

Are you on course? In order to know if you are on course, as we said in Chapter One, you need to know where you are going. For anyone who hikes, sails, flies or travels from point A to point B, you know that it is critical to stay on course. You know that while being one degree off course may not matter in the short run, it makes a huge difference in the long run. If you are traveling from Boston to San Francisco and you are just one degree off course, you will end up 55 miles from your intended destination. ***Most of us are more than one degree off course from being the man we aspire to be***. What will you do to stay on course? Like a compass, what tool do you use regularly to keep you on course?

It is essential that as a man you cultivate your self-discipline and continue to do so throughout your life. You must know where you are, where you are going, prepare yourself for the journey, and use the requisite tools to stay on course. Finally, your actions should never be conditional on the outcome obtained, but instead they must cause of the outcome you intend.

Security and Significance

There are many ways to describe the differences between the basic needs of men and women. In his book, *The Marriage Builder*, Dr. Larry Crabb advocates that a woman's primary need is for security and that a man's primary need is for significance. This is compatible and consistent with a woman's need for love and a man's need for respect. A man finds significance in his legacy and a woman finds security in her relationships. As a husband and a father, a significant part of your legacy is how you care for your wife and children. If you do well, your children will thrive and that will be a source of eternal joy. However, if you fail, it will be a source of profound grief when you see how your character, behavior, your very example has harmed them in perhaps irreversible ways. The most profound gut-wrenching grief I have ever witnessed was seeing a man finally acknowledge and accept how his leaving his wife harmed his children at a time when he could no longer do anything about it. For him this was overwhelming agony. I have witnessed this in other men enough times that I will never forget this valuable lesson.

Be Patient and Give it Time

It took time for your marriage to go off-course; it happened a little bit each day over a long period. You should expect that it may take just as much time and -- depending on the level of damage and hurt -- even longer to restore your marriage. You should not expect to make a few changes to your behavior and have the slate wiped clean. It will take some time for your wife to trust that these changes in character and behavior are permanent. Just bear in mind that your wife may forgive you, but she will never forget. In some cases, it may in fact get worse before it gets better. There are two dynamics at play that could contribute to this. First, feeling a new sense of security she may relax and release pent-up frustration, emotion, or negative feelings. This is good for her. Second, having been hurt once before, she will fervently test your resolve to ensure that the change is genuine, to ensure it is not just a transient fad. Don't be afraid, steadfast determination and perseverance will win out in the end. She will give you a second chance, be patient. If you are willing to forgive and accept her and she is as well, your relationship could be restored in significantly less time.

Be Responsible

Throughout this book, I have challenged you to be responsible. It is the only way for you to successfully navigate the challenges of marriage, fatherhood and life itself. If you have the courage to hold yourself to this standard, it will pay amazing dividends in all areas of your life. The most important benefits will manifest themselves in the quality of your life with your wife and children. Furthermore, your children will reflect this in their own character and behavior.

The alternative is painfully less desirable, as the sins of the father will be manifested in their sons. In his book, *Understanding the Divorce Cycle: The Children of Divorce in their Own Marriages*, Nicholas Wolfinger found that men whose fathers have affairs and get divorced are 40% more likely to do the same. Another interesting fact is that the rate increases to 91% if the father marries someone else after divorcing his wife.

Be mindful of the company that you keep. You are at greater risk of getting divorced if your friends get divorced. As to whether divorce might be 'contagious', Rose McDermott and her colleagues at Brown University "found that study participants were 75% more likely to become divorced if a friend is divorced and 33% more likely to end their marriage if a friend of a friend is divorced." [8]

In addition to the excuses you may use to justify your failure, you may find yourself using your friends' failures to justify your own. "If Bob and Mary couldn't keep it together, then how could I expect that we could?"

Conversely, if you do well, your best qualities will be mirrored in your sons and sought by your daughters when they chose their husbands. You have the power to establish a new standard for the men of your lineage: for your sons, and their sons, and so on for generations to come. You can create a new legacy by your commitment to being responsible for the quality of your character in your marriage, your family, and in your service to your community.

Pay attention to yourself, be mindful of your behaviors; your children are watching.

Ownership

Ownership - now many of you may not have given this word much thought. However, ownership is a critically important concept. Think about how you care for those things that you own when compared to those things you rent. Ownership embodies a level of care and concern for the future welfare of the things you own. How do you treat your car, home, or even a pair of skis compared to the same items as rentals? If you are like most men, ownership creates a personal obligation to preserve the value of something for future use. How you care for the things that you own is ultimately a reflection of you and your character. Ownership is beyond just being

[8] http://www.pewresearch.org/fact-tank/2013/10/21/is-divorce-contagious/ October 2013

responsible for something. Your ownership drives your actions as you allow it to require sacrifices from you.

Ownership extends well beyond physical assets or possessions. You can and should take ownership of a purpose or cause. If you are dedicated to and honorably serve your purpose, this will lead you to do your part and possibly even your best at it. Ownership is beyond dedication. When a man takes ownership of a cause, he declares 'the buck stops here, I am responsible for everything.' With ownership, you become invested in the mission and the very livelihood of the cause. And when you take ownership of something, it will cause you, compel you, to acquire and develop the character traits and skills needed to successfully serve this purpose. It will shape and mold you. No longer can you give into the "I can't" or "I am not (blank) enough." Your excuses will be pushed away by your ownership. May I remind you from Chapter Three, it is your obligations and responsibilities as a man that drive the development of your character. It doesn't happen any other way!

The 7 Ps, also Known as Be Prepared

One of my father's favorite mantras was: "Proper Prior Planning Prevents Piss Poor Performance." Also known as the Seven P's, it is a more provocative and a more memorable way of saying "BE PREPARED"! (The Boy Scouts' founding motto for more than a century!)

As I have suggested earlier, good men fail every day, not because they are bad or lack honorable intentions; they fail because they have no idea what they are doing and lack the mindset needed to succeed! They exhibit all of the bad behaviors and all too few of the good ones. I didn't know much at all when I got married at 23 years of age; but the one thing I *did* know...is that I didn't know what I was doing! I had never been married and I knew that I didn't have good examples to follow. This mindset was essential for me to expend the effort required to learn what I have over the past 35 years. Much of what I have learned I have laid out before you in this book and I earnestly intend that it will provide you the keys to create a magical life. With this guide, you can establish a firm foundation and quickly create a marriage that will last a lifetime. But you must be open to change and willing to do the work: **for nothing ventured, nothing gained.** While I have specifically referenced some, I have included many more resources for you in the appendix. I urge you to make a practice of reading books, listening to broadcasts, podcasts or audio tapes on this subject. Engage a mentor, so you may develop your own experience and understanding and learn from those who have successfully navigated these waters before you. In doing so, you will be feeding the "Good Dog" and keeping yourself on track.

If you are willing to develop your character and understanding to become a master craftsman in your role as a husband, then the rewards will be truly priceless.

The Scout Motto – Be Prepared

Continuing on this theme, I have spent more than two decades developing the character of young men through my commitment and dedication to Boy Scouts. I can assure you that the tools of scouting are essential tools for all men regardless of whether or not you were ever a Boy Scout. The tools are: The Scout Oath, The Scout Law, The Motto, and the Slogan. The Scout Oath is a promise a Scout makes to himself about his conduct. The Scout Law describes a set of qualities or character traits that governs a Scout's behavior. The Slogan "Do a Good Turn Daily" reminds a Scout to do something meaningful each day for others, and the Scout Motto is "Be Prepared." As Scoutmaster, I can't tell you how difficult it is to lead Scouts to adopt our Motto. But when they do, their experience, impact and outcomes are significantly better. This is true in every aspect of their life, whether it is for the next scouting trip, their next test in school, or in their daily life, as it is true for you.

Preparation begins with a plan: where you are going, who you are going with, how long it will take. Two project management adages are relevant here. The first is "Plan the work and then work the Plan." The second is "If you fail to plan, then you plan to fail." Now let's take a closer more personal look.

You demonstrate you care for something or someone through the depth of your preparation.

If you want to know what you really care about, pay attention to how you prepare for those things. How do you prepare for each day, doing your work, for a date, or a vacation? Since a man is generally doing what is important to him, it is worth paying attention to how you spend your time.

It is equally important to remember that each experience you have throughout your life will prepare you for what's next.

Be Generous

Above all things, be generous with your wife. The Golden Rule is do unto others as you would have them do unto you. If you wish for your wife to be generous with you, then set the example and be generous. Take care of her and do a really good job. As a father, if you take great care of your wife, she will take great care of your children and do it better than you. Conversely, if you are stingy with her, then your children will suffer, and, worse, you will be teaching your children to treat her the same way and everyone suffers for generations to come.

The First and Final Charge

If you can train yourself to be strong and disciplined, then the rewards will be great. It is when you are tested, tempted, challenged or stressed that your true nature and real character are revealed. How you respond to life's challenges reveals a lot about you and your character. How do you respond when life requires something of you?

Are you a man who makes excuses, who rationalizes when you compromise your character? One who blames others for your adversities? Do you argue for your weaknesses and why you can't do something? Or, are you a man who takes responsibility with courage, determination, patience, perseverance, and generosity? Notice that I said 'takes', rather than 'accepts.' You accept responsibility for what is your responsibility, but you take responsibility when it is something you aren't otherwise responsible for.

At the end of your days, when all is said and done, when nothing more can be done and no longer can anything be *undone*, what will those that knew you say about the man, husband, father, colleague, counselor, comforter, guardian, leader, and friend you have been? I hope you will be content with the outcome and I charge you to do your very best! Be the best husband and father you can be.

Key Thoughts

- Your true character is revealed when you are tested.
- Love remains and always will be…a VERB!
- Is good, good enough? Your family deserves your very best!
- Good is the enemy of great.
- Time will tell.

Recommended Actions

- Invest the time required to become a great husband.
- Be Objective.
- Celebrate your marriage, always and in all ways.
- Always and in every way, do your very best!
- Lead by example.

Questions for Reflection

1. Where are you settling for good enough? Where it is not good enough?

2. What tools and disciplines will you use to keep yourself on the path of living as the best man you can be?

3. At the end of your days, when it is all said and done, when nothing more can be done or undone, what will those who know you say about the man, husband, father, colleague, counselor and friend you have been?

4. What standards will you hold yourself to?

Appendix

"More good stuff"

Guiding Principles

1. The measure of a man is his willingness to be responsible for that which he is not responsible for.
2. The performance of your skills must exceed the opinion of your skills.
3. The easiest mess to clean up is the one you don't make!
4. How would things be if everyone was doing what I am doing?
5. The moment before a man willingly gives into his addiction, he must tell himself a lie!
6. Be careful what you look for: you will surely find it.
7. Never use the actions or inactions of another as an excuse for your own!
8. The way a man does the little things is the way he does the big things.
9. You demonstrate your care through the depth of your preparation.
10. It is the thought that you have a choice that creates the doubt, *no choice equals no doubt.*
11. Every decision in your life has already been made by the man you aspire to be. Your job is to keep quiet and do what he tells you to do.
12. Ascribe to others the best possible intentions, and acknowledge your true intentions.
13. I'd rather be wrong and do the right thing, than be right and do the wrong thing!
14. It is your obligations and responsibilities as a man, honorably served, that drive the development of your character!
15. The way to be the man that God calls you to be, is to do what that man requires of you unreservedly.
16. How a man behaves in his marriage is the most accurate reflection of his character.
17. The only way to be a good father is to be a great husband.
18. Your wife finds her security in the depth of your self-discipline.

19. If your children don't think that you are the most disciplined man on the planet, then you have work to do.
20. The only way to take care of your children is to take care of the community that you will leave them.
21. The problems of the world are not a result of the actions of the bad, but the silence of the good.
22. Gratitude is the seed of generosity.
23. You are always leading; your job is to be responsible for the quality of your leadership.
24. To become the master of your life, you must become the master of your attitude.
25. Develop the courage to allow other men to push you past where you quit on your own.
26. No man knows what his best really is, he only knows what his last best was.
27. Be careful, the life you lead just may be your own.
28. How would things be if everyone was doing what I am doing?

Recommended Resources

Books

The Bible, New King James Version (1975)

The Winning Attitude (1992) by John C. Maxwell

King, Magician, Lover, Warrior (1991) by Douglas Gillette & Robert Moore

The Way of the Superior Man – A man's guide to women, work, and sexual desire (1997) by David Deida

Iron John (1990) by Robert Bly

Seven Habits of Highly Effective People by Stephen Covey

Make Your Bed: 10 Life Lessons from a Navy SEAL (2017) by Admiral William H. McRaven

The 5 Love Languages: The Secret to Love that Lasts by Gary Chapman

The Love Dare by Alex Kendrick and Stephen Kendrick

The Surprising Secrets of Highly Happy Marriages by Shaunti Feldhahn

Hedges - Loving Your Marriage Enough to Protect It by Jerry Jenkins

The First Five Years of Marriage: Launching a Lifelong, Successful Relationship (2007) by Phillip J. Swihart, Wilford Wooten

The Marriage Builder: Creating True Oneness to Transform Your Marriage by Larry Crabb

The Keys to the Kingdom by Alison Armstrong

Change your Heart and Change your Life (2012) by Gary Smalley

How to Win Friends & Influence People by Dale Carnegie

The Autobiography of Benjamin Franklin by Benjamin Franklin

Broadcasts / Podcast

Focus on the Family – www.focusonthefamily.com

Movies

Courageous (2011)

Fireproof (2008)

Pay it Forward (2000)

Dead Poets Society (1989)

Taming of the Shrew (1967)

Workshops / Videos

Mark Gungor: Laugh Your Way to a Better Marriage – DVD

Mark Gungor - Sex is what men want from women.wmv - Youtube

www.ingramcontent.com/pod-product-compliance
Lightning Source LLC
Chambersburg PA
CBHW021504090426
42739CB00007B/451
* 9 7 8 1 9 5 1 8 0 5 2 6 5 *